# SOME HURTS

# ARE BEYOND

# TEARS

## By Glennette

## Nelson

# Acknowledgments

Birth is never easy, be it spiritual or natural. It's traumatic to the one being born and the one giving birth. So you can only imagine the pain and trauma in trying to birth into existence this literary baby. For seven years I've been pregnant. At times I thought this baby had died within me, but every now and then it would give a kick to let me know it was still alive and almost ready to be born. It was just waiting on me to push. Sometimes there are complications in the birthing process, and you need help in the delivery. I thank God for having sent a midwife in the form of Lynette Kea Jones to help me with the birthing process. You have been such an inspiration throughout this whole journey. You've challenged my views on love and made me an even better writer. I couldn't have done this without you. This is just the beginning.

I want to thank my cousins Shameka White-Vital (we've been rolling together since we were eleven; you are a joy, and we have a bond that neither time nor distance can break) and Janetta "Boobie" Randle for always being willing to answer the phone when I called, just to listen to me vent and then give me honest feedback whether I wanted to hear it or not. I love you both. For years I was hurt, angry, bitter, and untrusting except to a few who had been through the fire with me, and even with them I kept myself at a distance, just in case. But who knew that moving to Texas would catapult me into my destiny and that God would use a group of people whom I never saw coming to lay siege to the walls I had built and break through the defenses to my heart?

To Felica Alford-Booker: Girl, you have been a friend indeed. You have worked tirelessly behind the scenes, never asking for anything. You have helped me out of many a tough spot. Love you.

To Ashley Parramore, Mia Moss, and Deneice Cobb: You three have been my rocks. You've seen me at my worst and still loved me. You've encouraged me, fussed at me, and defended and protected me even though I'm the eldest. You've shown me what real sisterhood truly means.

To Pastor Laura O'Neal: There's not enough room to tell you what you mean to me. You are sister, momma, and friend all wrapped up in one. You have been there every step of the way in my spiritual growth, poking and prodding me to keep growing even when I didn't want to. You've bailed me out too many times to count and treated me like one of your own. I will love you to infinity and beyond. (Even though I'm still a little salty about you hanging up in my face that one time.)

To Mother Debra Small-Parramore: You're another one who took me in like I was your own. Your approach was a little more of the tough-love method. You've fussed and pushed me to never accept anything less than what was best for me. At one of my lowest points, you were there. When I didn't have any food, you took me to the grocery store and just said, "Shop." I will love you forever.

To Elder Michelle Riser Coleman:
When I first came to the ministry and
was overwhelmed by the sheer size
and was ready to leave, you took it
upon yourself to try to mentor me. I
don't think you realized the
humongous task you were taking on.
Well, after sixteen years I've finally
decided to let the mentoring take.
You have been such a dear friend
over the years. You've been
transparent with me on many
occasions so that I could see I wasn't
alone in some of life's struggles.
Love you.

To Pastor Darrell and First Lady
LaTonja Blair: Pastor Darrell, you sir
were a God send. When I first came
to the ministry I was a mess, but you
looked pass that and loved me as
only a big brother can love a bratty
sister. You have encouraged me and
corrected me as only family can.

LaTonja, Thank you so much for all
the genuine hugs, smiles, and prayers
through the years. You welcomed a
stranger into your home and family
and turned me into a sister.

To Pastor Eric and First Lady Cassandra Paul: Elder Paul, you have been the epitome of a brother. You have listened to me in all my rambling. You have nodded and smiled like I was making all the sense in the world, even when I didn't make sense to myself. Your advice on relationships has been invaluable, whether I listened or not. You're the big brother whom I've always wanted but never had.

Cassandra, you have been such an inspiration. You have let me be me and loved me through all my antics. You encouraged me to dance. You've helped me grow creatively and opened my eyes to so many different things. You've laughed with me and played with me, even though we were supposed to be listening to pastor preach.

To Minister Miesha Keaton: It has been amazing watching you flourish and grow with God, but even more amazing is that with all that God is doing in your life, you still take the time out to encourage me in all my endeavors. You come out and support me in both word and deed. You're a beauty on the outside as well as the inside.

To Minister Inga Trapp: You are my friend for real. You take everything that I dish out and return it with love. You do with me what I missed out on while growing up. You play with me. That little girl who has been locked away for years—you let her come out, and you let her play until she tires herself out, even when it is inconvenient to you. You wear so many different hats but still have time and energy to cater to the little lost girl in me. We both thank you.

To Charles Ashley: Thank you for taking a chance on a stranger, hearing God, and sowing into my life, and thank you for trying to teach me to focus. (I'm still working on it.)

To Portia Hicks, Emmanuel Obeng-Mensah, and Deedria Patterson Williams: Thanks for the long talks and encouragement and believing my story could change lives.

Last, but definitely not least, I want to thank my pastors, Dr. Sherman C.

Gee and Co-Pastor Otonya Allen.
Pastor Allen, you came into my life
at a time when my trust in people
and belief in myself was at an all-
time low, at a time when I didn't
really want to live but was too scared
to die. You took in this rough-
around-the-edges, scared little girl,
and with God's help you molded her
and shaped her into a woman of
substance, strong enough to face her
past and use it as a testimony to
show that God is a healer and not
only physically—he heals souls,
minds, and spirits too. I am a
witness. Without you, I would have
never had the courage to tell my
story, not because it didn't need to be
told, but because I didn't feel worthy
of telling it. Pastor Allen, over the
years you have sowed so much into
my life that if I live to be a hundred,
I'll never be able to repay you, so I
talked to God, and he said, "Put it on
his tab." You and Co-Pastor Otonya
show me who I want to be in God's
kingdom—strong and sure. Co-
Pastor Otonya, thank you for loving
me and accepting me with my flaws
and all and sharing your family with
me. I never doubt your love for me;

know that I love you from the bottom of my heart.

# Dedication

In loving memory of:

Georgia Mae Roberson, who loved me unconditionally and never judged me. She was and will always be the mommy of my heart.

Linda Harris: You were a great sister. You had the bossiness down pat. I miss you.

Betty "Janetta" Chiles: Our relationship was different, but real. We had our own way of loving each other, and I miss you every day.

Vergie Randle: When no one else would, you did. Thank you for trying.

To my son, Marcus Nelson: This book is dedicated to you. It's not how things start; it's how they end. I love you so much. I know how to do it now. You are mine, and I am yours, and there's nothing we can't do. Never stop reaching for the stars.

# Foreword

*Some Hurts Are Beyond Tears* is a transparent, poignant, and riveting journey into the life of a now-young-adult African American woman who takes us on a roller-coaster ride through the American foster-care system. As she bares her heart and soul, Glennette Nelson allows the reader to experience her despair as she plummets hopelessly into the system, from one group home and foster parent to another. Her candor, anger, bitterness, and, ultimately, her spiritual and moral awakening will have you despising her reckless and sometimes-violent behavior while, at the same time, cheering for her as she morphs into a courageous, mature, caring young woman who transforms her anger into passion and compassion for others who are imprisoned in the system that she narrowly escaped.

You will laugh, cry, shout, and cringe as you feel Glennette's pain and watch her moments of precocious banality turn into a thoughtful, meaningful, and impassioned life whose purpose is to give to those who have no hope and about whom few care, unless, of course, they have been there themselves.

This book is not just a story; it is a call to action for all humanity to understand that our pain is, indeed, connected to our passion and that our passion, once channeled in the right direction, fuels our purpose. Passion unleashed without purpose is a very dangerous force.

As you embark upon Glennette's journey, may you rediscover why you are on the planet, and may you move beyond whatever has caused you pain to embrace your purpose. Glennette's agonizing experiences chronicled within these pages are carefully and meticulously revealed in often-painstaking detail without excuse in order to help each of us understand the mentality and subculture that this system creates. Your glimpse into the life of one lost and abandoned child will, hopefully, empower you to understand and to help others who have no voice, no hope, too few advocates, and all too often no one who even cares.

*Some Hurts Are Beyond Tears* is a book of courage and compassion, trial and triumph, hurt and healing. As you open these pages and share Glennette's life story, may reading it be as cathartic for you as it was for me. May you come away from this book willing to hope again, to care again, and to try again and again and again until something, or someone, changes for the better. As you experience vicariously the difficult and painful memories of this brave young woman's past, remember that sometimes you have to go beneath the scars to reopen a wound in order for others to share in your healing.

Dr. Sherman C. Gee Allen

## Introduction

Foster care. The sound of those words should resonate with a peaceful and warm feeling throughout one's insides. It carries with it a nurturing and loving connotation.

However, movies such as the acclaimed *Antwone Fisher*, released in 2002, depict many of the horrifying realities of the foster-care system and the lifelong effects and permanent scarring left on the lives and minds of many children who are forced to endure the often-unproductive process of being bounced around from one home or family to another.

Using these experiences as launching pads for a better life and way of being, many children who survive this atrocity go on to become healthy, whole, and delivered men and women who want to use the empowerment of their survival to help others.

This is my motivation for writing this book and telling my story, because while that is my testimony today, it was not always my

outlook on life and my existence. As you
will discover as you read about my
experience in the foster-care system, it is my
hope that you either become inspired to
make a positive difference in a child's life or
that you will have compassion for a child
you know who's gone through traumatic life
changes.

Many people end up in the foster-care
system for a variety of reasons.[1] At the age
of two, singer and songwriter Cher was
placed in care when her mother became too
ill to care of her. When Cher was able to

return home again, her grandparents were a major part of her upbringing while her mother was struggling.

Did you know that basketball great Alonzo Mourning was placed in the foster home of a family friend after a fallout with his parents following their divorce? Alonzo, or "Zo," was twelve and was already six feet tall when he went to his new home. Mourning practiced nonstop after he found basketball. He excelled in college and went on to win an NBA championship with the Miami Heat.

And then there was the late Steve Jobs (1955–2011), who was born in a time when mothers who had babies out of wedlock were looked down upon. He was adopted by a married couple soon after his birth. Steve was very bright but got into a lot of trouble, even getting expelled from school. I am in very good company on all counts.

Jobs was so smart, though, that he was able to skip a couple of grades and became very interested in electronics. He started assembling computers in his garage and was soon changing the computer world.

He was the cofounder and CEO of Apple.

Not all of the stories end up this way, and many of these children's stories are never told. As you can imagine, children in foster care experience high rates of child abuse, emotional deprivation, and physical neglect.

A study of foster children in Oregon and Washington State found that nearly one-third reported being abused by a foster parent or another adult in a foster home.

This usually resulted in unhealthy, disruptive, toxic, or illegal behaviors by those placed there. I was no exception. *But God!*

He had a plan for my life. In spite of my traumatic beginning and my foolish middle, God would have the final say by intervening with his grace and mercy. (**Jeremiah 29:11**: *"For I know the plans that I have for you, declares the LORD, plans for welfare and not for calamity to give you a future and a hope."*)

Through his son, my savior, Jesus Christ, God gave me new lease on life, a fresh start, and a focused and undeniable purpose. He allowed me to take all the emotional, physical, mental, and spiritual hurt derived from my life in foster care and be a lifeline for someone else. To go beyond the hurt, to being healed holistically and living my life to the fullest.

I may not sing like Cher, dunk like Zo, or transform technology like Steve Jobs, but I will be the best me I can as I live my life to please the God of my salvation and help as many children and survivors as I can. (**Psalm 27:10**: *"For my father and my* *mother have forsaken me, But the Lord will*

*take me up.")*

## The Beginning

There were times growing up that I just didn't care. Who am I kidding? I never cared, not really. People have said, "Look five years in the future, and tell me where you see yourself."

I was never able to see that image, because I thought on some level that I would never make it.

During my teen-age years I lived my life full speed ahead, never thinking about the consequences, never learning from my mistakes, never believing that there was anything special about me or any real purpose for my being here. I've come to realize that by putting my thoughts and memories on paper, that pain and heartache can be relived, and if you're not careful, the pain can be much worse the second time around.

Before you read any further, understand that the things I did and the decisions I made hurt me so much more than they hurt anyone else, and I understand that my actions impacted the lives of others. Although you may be tempted to judge, remember that

only God can judge me.

## We Are *"Family"*

Abuse was the reason I ended up being
made to leave the only place I knew of as
home. "Abuse" is such an ugly word, but
I've seen my fair share of it through the
years, whether it was self-inflicted or at the
hands of others. From what I can tell, abuse
seems to run down through the maternal line
of my family—from my grandmother to my
mother and on to me.

Although my grandmother had children
from a previous marriage, my mother was

13

the only child of Rev. Willie and Beatrice Drew. She was the baby, spoiled and loved by her parents. A preacher's kid.

But as we know, all the love and good teaching in the world doesn't make anyone any less apt to fall into a pit of bad mistakes. She had my older brother, Dontay, at sixteen. I was born when she was twenty-one years old, and my younger brother, Glenn James, by age twenty-five.

At the tender age of five, my definition of "family" was determined by the events my little mind could understand at the time. It was all I knew, and I didn't have any other point of reference to tell me that it wasn't normal.

I am not sure of the emotional state of my parents' relationship, but I do know that when my father came into the picture, things got real ugly, really fast. I never understood how a mother could stand aside and let a piece of herself be abused. And I have never been able to understand how a person can hurt the person whom they claim to love.

15

But that's exactly what happened. My father also abused my brother and would beat him so badly that, to this day, my brother's back bears the scars from a grown man's rage.

A rage so furious I was sure that one day he was going to kill my brother, but my grandmother stepped in and took custody of Dontay.

My parents fought a lot, and there was plenty of screaming, yelling, punching, black eyes, and bloody noses, not to mention the drugs and alcohol that instigated much of this behavior and lack of self-control.

At times when my parents weren't together, my mom would bring strange men around, and we saw my dad less and less after he moved out, but he would come by and see us and sometimes even bring gifts.

We fell on hard times, as money was short and an eviction was always on our heels. I remember when my father came to visit me and Glenn James and he decided to take us to the Magic Mountain amusement park.

My parents argued about it because my mother didn't want to release us to my father because he wasn't sober. I cried aloud about how badly I wanted to go, but Glenn James seemed not to care one way or the other, and I don't believe he was even old enough to understand.

I, on the other hand, was six years old, and all I wanted to do was spend time with my daddy.

As usual, the argument grew hot and intense, and my dad hit my mother in the head with the telephone receiver, grabbed us up, and put us in the car, and off we went.

Now that I am older, I often wonder, did he fall asleep behind the wheel or was he trying to kill all of us? Either way, we never made it to Magic Mountain. Instead he drove off the side of a mountain, and it was nothing but God's grace that I am alive to share my story today. I woke up upside down in the car with darkness all around me. It seemed like forever before anybody came to help us. They had to rappel down on ropes to pull us out of the wreckage.

My brother didn't have a single scratch, and all I had was a bloody nose from where I hit the dashboard. For us to not have been wearing seat belts, you know that was God!

My father, on the other hand, almost went through the windshield, losing the use of one of his eyes because of the shattered glass.

He was rushed to the hospital, and we were placed in a foster home until they could find my mother. It took them a week to locate her. Once we were reunited with her, she took us to the hospital to see our father for

what would be the last time for ten years.

## Tulsa, *Not* OK!

My mother packed up what little possessions we had and we drove to Tulsa, Oklahoma. She told us that we were going to see her sister, our aunt. When we finally got there, it was nothing like what I expected. My aunt had five children whom she was raising alone. I'm pretty sure she didn't need two more mouths to feed. But I am so glad that she did it.

My mom had me and my brother Glenn James bring our belongings into the house.

Then she told us she would be right back after making a run to the corner store. We waited and waited by that front door, but she didn't come back. I was so heartsick. I didn't know these people. I don't care who they said they were to me. I wanted my mom to come back. Every day I prayed and prayed for God to send my mom back home. I was in a place where nothing was familiar, and all in the space of a few weeks I had lost my entire family. No daddy. No mom. No grandma.

The most important people to a child's psyche were gone. Every night I cried myself to sleep until slowly but surely, like most children in my predicament, I started to adjust, even though my behavior was not always the best.

For example, even though I would eat the same food as my cousins did, I would wake up in the middle of the night and sneak into the kitchen to steal food, or I would take the scraps that we had saved for the dogs and, instead of feeding it to them, I would eat them myself.

When we would go to football games at the high school, I would eat food off the ground. There were times while at school, the janitor would catch me eating out of the trash can.

I wish I could explain my reasoning for doing those things, but I couldn't then, and I can't now.

I have to say that though there were some bad times, like the time one of the guys in the neighborhood asked me and my little brother if we wanted to play a game. He then led us into the garage, and he sat us down on this old, flowery ratty couch, he blindfolded us and said we were going to do a tasting game, and I was going first. He told me he was going to put something in my mouth, and I was to tell him what I tasted, but not to bite down. And because I always wanted something to eat, I said OK. He told me to open my mouth but remember not to bite down, and if I could tell him what it was, he'd give me and Glenn James a treat. I really wanted that treat, so I tried to peek through the gap in the blindfold.

I couldn't really see, so when he put it
against my lips, I licked and tasted ketchup;
when I told him my answer, he said I was
right. He said, "One more," as he turned to
do whatever it was he was doing. I rubbed
my eyes and tugged the blindfold down a
little. That's when he said to try this flavor. I
could see what he was putting against my
lips, it wasn't food. As I sat there, he rubbed
his penis against my lips and told me to
taste, and as he tried to stick it in my mouth,
I did what he kept telling me not to do. I bit
it, jerked off the blindfold, grabbed my little

27

brother, and ran like the devil himself was after us. My brother was crying because he couldn't see, and I was dragging him, and I was crying because I knew that wasn't something little kids were supposed to do, and I didn't want to get in trouble. So I kept quiet.

There were good times too. There was a blackberry tree on the side of my aunt Vergie's house, and we would pick the berries, wash them with saltwater, and eat till our mouths were all shades of purple. One time I must have eaten too many berries, because I got real sick. Me and my cousin Boobie sometimes slept in the same bed, and the night I got sick, I was sleeping with her. The berries had my stomach all torn up, and I was so sick I pooped all on her. She was not happy!

I remember doing cheers on the corner under the streetlights. We would ride each other on the handlebars of the bikes that had no brakes, so we had to stop them with our feet and hope to God that nobody was hurt when they fell off the handlebars—which was most of the time.

I had lost the only family I knew, but I had gained some cousins who would love me no matter what in the years to come.

Almost a year to the day after leaving us, my mother came back, but she didn't come alone. She had gotten married during her time away. She told us that we were moving to Washington, DC, where her new husband had this great job and a big, wonderful house. There was the promise of having my own room and everything that I had ever wanted. I was torn because I had finally settled into my new environment and I would miss my cousins, but I finally had

what I had been praying for every day: for

my mom to come back. Somehow, I just

knew that with her back, everything would

be right with my world again and that only

good things could happen going forward.

Ah, the innocence of childish thinking.

**Betrayed**

When we made it to Washington, DC, there was no job! No big house! And no safety in the arms of my mother. Her new husband wasn't the loving stepfather he portrayed himself to be.

We lived in a pay-by-the-week motel. I was surprised to see there were quite a few other families who lived there too, but not many had children. So I would have no one to play with when I would get put out of the room so they could "do grown-up stuff."

To keep myself busy, I would climb a tree that stood at the back of the motel. The tree was so high, climbing it felt like an adventure. I never even thought about falling. All I thought about was that if maybe I got as high as I could, I would be closer to God, and maybe he would come see about me. In the meantime, the tree would have to do, and I enjoyed being cradled in the arms of its branches. I was safe there. No one could touch me.

My stepfather didn't work. Instead, he sent my mom out to make money. Not having much work experience, I could only imagine what she had to do to earn it, and when she didn't bring to him what he felt that she should, he would beat her.

I remember a time my mom sent me and my little brother outside to play. I slipped back to the motel room, and as I came closer, I could hear him talking loudly and my mother crying. I cracked open the door to the room and peered in to find my mother laying across the bed naked and my stepfather beating her with a belt.

## Some Hurts Are Beyond Tears

I turned and ran as fast as I could and climbed my tree. Nobody could get to me there. With all the violence going on around me at nine years old, I reverted back to wetting the bed and stealing food.

My mom got so mad at me once after I wet the bed and blamed it on my brother that she started beating me with an extension cord when I wouldn't stop screaming because of the pain. (I know I shouldn't have blamed him, but surely my actions didn't call for all that.)

What happened to my mommy, the one who used to hug and love on me all those years ago? What happened to the mother who nurtured me right under her heart, who whispered to me that she'd protect me and never let anything hurt me? Where did she go? This new mother was different. She wrapped the extension cord around my throat and started choking me until I thought I was going to die. The only reason I blamed my brother is that I knew my mom and step-father loved him more than me. He never got in trouble. He could do no wrong.

They babied him, but me they just tolerated.
I begin to act out at school just to get
attention. I started stealing, and because I
felt like I was always hungry, I begin
stealing food or begging strangers.

I stole a piece of bologna out of the cooler
we had in our motel room while everyone
was gone, but before I could eat it all, my
mom came back, so I ran in the bathroom
and stuck it into a hole in the wall. When my
mother went into the cooler, she noticed
some of the lunch meat was gone and of
course she asked me about it, but of course I

lied, because I knew I was going to get a whipping. It didn't matter to them that I was hungry.

When my stepfather got back to the motel room and she told him what had happened, he got two small pots and filled them with water. He made me get on my knees and hold one pot in each hand in a cross-like position, and he said that if I moved, he was going to beat me. I knew he wasn't just saying that, because I had seen him in action. As I knelt there with my mother and brother looking on, he started to throw

things at me to get me to drop the pots of
water, and of course, because I was a little
girl with no strength in my arms, it was only
a matter of time before I did.

When I dropped them, he grabbed me up by
my ponytail, and he grabbed the belt that he
always used for whipping occasions. It was
a thick, brown leather belt with a silver
buckle the size of a grown man's fist, and
when he beat me, he never held anything
back, and he never cared where the belt
landed on my small body. The next day my
mom and step-father decided to go on a

39

"family" outing to the lake, but they said I couldn't go, so they left me at the motel all day. They locked me out of the room with no water and no food, and the only place to use the bathroom was outside. When they finally came back, most people were already in the bed for the night. I was thirsty and hungry, but they sent me to bed with nothing.

I remember thinking, "What was it about me that they hated so much? What could I have done in my short life that could cause people to think that it was all right to mistreat me?"

40

That was my life for months: walking on eggshells, trying not to attract the attention of my mom or step-father.

One day when I had to ask my step-father for something, he told me not to call him "daddy" because he wasn't. What was I supposed to call him, then? It's not like I could call him by his first name.

I tried to disappear into myself. I went to school and played outside. I felt safest when my mom or step-father would put me out of the room.

Then one morning I woke up to find that my mom and my little brother had gone. It seemed a little strange because they were always there when I woke up, but not on this morning. It was just me and my stepfather. Have you ever gotten that dreadful feeling in the pit of your stomach?

As I sat up in my bed, he was in the other bed just staring at me. He told me to come over to him. I have heard it said that all animals have an inbred sense of self-preservation, and even at that young age, I possessed that sense in spades. I was scared

42

to go to him but even more afraid not to. He told me to get up on the bed, so I climbed up on the bed, my little body trembling, and he pulled my nightgown up, exposing my small body, and he just looked at me. I wanted to cover myself so badly, but his look froze me with fear.

He took his finger and gently started running his finger from my throat to my pubic area. The gentleness of his touched terrified me because he was never gentle with me. He told me he wanted to show me what boys were going to want to do to me when I got

43

older. He started touching me with his hands, and then he pulled his penis out and started rubbing it between my legs. Oh God, I thought, please save me! (**Psalm 88:15**: *"I was afflicted and about to die from my youth on; I suffer Your terrors; I am overcome."*)

Tears were falling from my eyes like a flood that could wipe out a small city. "Where's my mommy?" I thought. "Why is he doing this to me." God didn't save me that day.

I just laid there and stared in a deep gaze at that dingy ceiling and imagined I was a bird that lived high up in the clouds where nothing could touch me. I don't even remember if I made a sound, maybe because it wouldn't have made a difference.

This man who wanted to make sure I knew he wasn't my father treated me and my existence as if I were expendable and disposable. His actions set in motion the beginning of toxic and contaminated sexual relations. (They were hardly relationships.)

After it was over, I was never the same physically or mentally. I know in time many

45

wounds heal, but mentally and emotionally some of those wounds never go away. The scars remain. Tattoos can mask, but they don't erase the pain, and the tracks of my tears are forever etched in a dark place.

He got more hateful after that day. I couldn't look at him, and I couldn't talk to him, and my mother, she didn't want to hear anything I had to say when I tried to tell her what happened.

Something shriveled up and died in me. My mother, the one who had carried me in her womb for nine months, didn't love me

enough to protect me. Not long after that, I

came home from school to find that my

mom had a suitcase packed for me. She took

me and that suitcase down to the welfare

office and left me there.

## New Beginning...Yeah, Right. Next!

I was placed in a foster home in care of Miss Jordan. She was an older, black lady. She was nice, but I just wanted to go home. I didn't care how horrible it was; I just wanted my mom. They say the ability of children to bounce back after trauma is remarkable. I was proof positive. Even after she had just abandoned me, threw me out like last month's trash, all I wanted was a nurturing hug and acceptance from my mother.

I was so tired of being with people I didn't know. I was so scared, surrounded by people I didn't know in a place so unfamiliar. I felt so alone.

I found a phone book and looked until I found the name of the motel where my mother was. I called her and begged her to come get me. I promised that I would be good; I'd do anything if she would just come back and get me.

I cried until I thought my chest would crack open from the pressure as she hung up in my face. Miss Jordan was a nice lady, but she wasn't my family. She was an older lady and very sweet, doing what she thought was right. I'm pretty sure that when she took me in, she was expecting a semi normal, just-glad-to-be-in-a-nice-safe-home kind of girl. But what she got was something altogether different.

You would think I'd be grateful to be in a house, to have plenty to eat and not be scared to go to sleep in fear of waking up with a grown man leaning over me, touching me in ways I wasn't meant to know or

50

understand at my age. But even there I didn't feel safe. But as with most anything you start fitting in, adapting, and getting used to things, Miss Jordan made sure that we went to church, a tiny Pentecostal congregation in Baltimore, Maryland. It was a different type of church than I'd ever been in before.

It was loud and boisterous and kind of scary! They sang, they danced, and they worshipped. Once during service, the preacher told us to close our eyes and just say "Thank you, Jesus" over and over again.

I remember closing my eyes on the front row and doing what the preacher had said. The next time I opened my eyes, I was on the other side of the room and a lady was rocking me back and forth. I had no idea what had happened. Scared the bejesus out of me; that's for sure. A couple there took a liking to me. They had one son about sixteen years old, and they always wanted me to sit with them after church. During the fellowship time in the dining area, their son would let me follow him around, and he was so nice to me until the time he took me upstairs to the Sunday-school room, where

he sat in a metal chair, grabbed my head,

and kissed me.

Not just a peck on the cheek; he stuck his

tongue in my month. It was disgusting!

I jumped up and ran out of the room, but

before I could get far, he grabbed my arm

and told me I better not say anything,

because they wouldn't believe me anyway. I

walked down the stairs just wanting to be

anywhere but there. That's when the Cain's

came to me and told me that they had great

news. I was coming to live with them.

Living with them wasn't all it was cracked

up to be. Their son hated my being there,

and I wasn't too thrilled about being around

him anymore myself. It was constant strife.

It got so bad that he decided he was going to

stay with his grandmother as long as I was

in the house, and of course with them loving

their son, it was decided that I would be the

one to leave, but first they had to find me

somewhere to go. Unwanted—again

**Will You Love Me?**

After leaving the Cains' foster home in
Baltimore, I somehow found my way back
to Tulsa. This time, though, instead of being
with my aunt Vergie, I ended up with my
cousin Betty Childs, whom everyone called
Janetta.

From the time I was eight years old until the
age of eleven, I was something she had to
get used to. Her daughter was grown and out
of the house. She was married to Charlie
Chiles. He was an amazing man. He was a

wonderful father figure. Maybe if he'd had a chance to raise me, I wouldn't have as many issues when it comes to the opposite sex. They say that the father is the first man a little girl loves, but what happens to a little girl's mind-set when there are numerous daddies with all different issues and personalities that pour into her life, none of them really good and some of them downright horrendous?

What kind of man does she end up loving?

I guess from the outside looking in, living with them I had a great life. I wore nice clothes; I had all the perks that a little girl could want. My own room decorated in Barbie pink with Barbie curtains and a pink Barbie bedspread. I had my own TV and video game. I went to the beauty shop every other week. I had it made!

So why was there still a big gaping hole in my chest? Janetta did her best. She gave me things I had never had, but it just wasn't enough. Christmases and birthdays were wonderful. One year for my birthday, I got a parakeet. It was beautiful. I kept trying to teach it how to talk, but that was a no-go. All it wanted to do was peck me every time I tried to pet it. The dang-on thing would just peck me. So every time it pecked me, I thumped it, until one day I think I thumped it too hard, because I looked in the cage and he was feet-up. I was a murderer of birds. Janetta swore up and down for years that I let that bird out and it got into some poison or something. I didn't have the heart to tell her I was a bird killer. So I let her think it.

For Christmas they got me a dog, a border collie. I named him Bear. (You'd think they'd have learned their lesson with the bird.)

She didn't understand me. To her I was ungrateful. I had everything I could want, so why was I still unhappy? I couldn't even begin to explain why I was still hopeless. When school started, since Charlie and Janetta worked a late shift, they didn't want me home alone, so they enrolled me in Walt Whitman Elementary. So every morning I would have to go to his mom's house and go to school from there and then wait for them to get off work in the evening to come pick me up. There were two other kids there, Tenisha and Shandell. They were Charlie's nieces.

Tenisha and I were almost the same age, but I was a grade ahead of her. Shandell was younger, but we all walked to school and played together. Like any family we had our ups and downs. We fussed and fought like all kids do at that age. Things were said. As an adult I understand that it wasn't being spiteful, just a child's observation. But just

60

like all kids, we would say and do hurtful
things. I remember once after I had started
calling Janetta and Charlie "Mom" and
"Dad," Tenisha said that they weren't really
my mom and dad. I remember being hurt
and angry. As children we don't realize that
some of the words we speak can have
lifelong effects. But there are good
memories, like the time Janetta cooked us
what we thought was smothered chicken.
She waited until we had eaten all the food
on our plate to tell us that we had eaten
smothered rabbit. Tenisha and I were

horrified. That Shandell, though, she asked

for seconds. We all went to the same school,

and we had to walk to school together, to

and from, though that didn't always happen.

For some reason a group of girls decided

that they would pick on me. So when I went

home to tell Janetta, she told me to tell those

girls that I wasn't scared of them.

She told me that you if you stood up to

bullies, they would leave you alone. Now, I

don't know what kind of bullies she had

dealt with, but the ones who bothered me

only got worse when I took her advice. After

62

I told them I wasn't afraid of them, I think
they took it as a personal goal to make sure I
learned to be scared of them. For two years,
every day, they chased me home. Two years.
Let's do the math. There are 365 days in a
year, minus weekends and holiday. That's
about 185 days times two, give or take a
few, when I had to worry about getting beat
on by my peers. Oh, and you know those
cousins, Tenisha and Shandell? Well, those
boogers left me to fend for myself! But
looking back, I can't blame them. Shandell
was younger than us, and Tenisha was

smaller, and the girls who picked on me—

well, let's just say they weren't small. It

never seemed to matter whether I dragged

my feet so they could go ahead of me or

whether I tried to beat them home.

Somehow or other they always got me. That

last year I tried to fight back. The first time

was with Lordette. She was really trying to

fight me, and I was really trying to get away.

Her brother gave her an umbrella—you

know, one of those big umbrellas with the

metal tip. Well, she chased me down the

street, beating at me with that thing. The

second time I tried to take up for myself was

against Melva. Once again they were

chasing me home and I was running like

Forrest Gump. She went to grab me and

somehow or other I grabbed her backpack

and slung her around, just trying to get

away, but she lost her balance and fell in the

street. I thought she was going to get hit by a

car, but I wasn't going to stay around and

watch. I was out of there. But everything

came to a head the last day of school my

fifth-grade year. Charlie was tired of my

running, and he told me it was time to stand

and fight—no more running. Janetta, on the other hand, said that if I got in a fight, she was going to beat my ass. Charlie said, "Betty, she's got to stand up for herself." So he told me what to do. He said that when whoever decides to fight me comes, ball up my fists and just start swinging like a windmill. He told me to keep my eyes open, and if she runs, don't chase her. I asked him why not. He said, "When you back a scared person into a corner, their whole mind-set changes and they can hurt you trying to get away." I didn't really understand that, since

I was scared and backed into a corner all the time, but I hadn't hurt anybody. But, hey, if he says don't chase her I wouldn't chase her. The day finally came. It was the last day of school, and Keisha was the one who had the pleasure of thinking she was going to beat me up. In her mind she thought this was going to be easy. Tenisha and Shandell had deserted me even though Charlie had sat us down earlier in the week and told us that we were cousins and cousins stick together. You fight one of us, you fight us all. I guess it sounded good in theory, but they weren't

67

having any of that. Later I found out that they went to find Janetta. Keisha and I were out there cussing each other like sailors, then she pushed me and I pushed her back and the fight was on. I held my head down like a bull about to charge, closed my eyes (as Charlie had told me not to do), balled up my fist, and started swinging. Today was my day to win, and winning I was. Then, all of a sudden, here comes this big, black woman pushing through the big crowd of kids with a big stick, cussing herself. You guessed it: Janetta. She grabbed me by my arm and dragged me out of the circle and pulled me toward the car, the whole time telling me, "Didn't I tell you not to be fighting?" As we got closer to the car, I could see Tenisha and Shandell looking out the window of the backseat, eyes as big as saucers. I think they were so used to me getting beat up, they did their best to help me without getting directly involved by getting Janetta.

The summer went by quickly. I stayed at home a lot watching TV and playing with my dog. Janetta and Charlie let me stay at home that summer instead of going to his mom's house. There was plenty of stuff to get into while they were at work. I'd let my dog, Bear, in the house to keep me company, and when it was almost time for them to get home from work, I'd put him back outside in his kennel. Life was pretty good. But like everything good in my life before, it soon came to an end. The week before I started school at Carver, a magnet middle school in Tulsa, I went to spend the weekend with my cousins at my aunt Vergie's house. That's when I found out some devastating news to my little mind.

My mom had a new baby girl. I didn't understand. Why would she go and have a new baby girl and she had already had me? Why wasn't I good enough? Why didn't anyone want to keep me? If my own mother didn't want me, there must have been something wrong with me, which meant it was only a matter of time before I lost this home I was in too.

By this time I had come to realize that my mom was never coming back for me. She didn't need me anymore. She had a new baby, a perfect baby. So I started acting out.

My grades at Carver started to drop, so I
forged my progress reports. I started stealing
from the girls in gym class, and I started
stealing money from home to buy candy to
give away at school. I stole a check from
Janetta and filled it out in pencil and tried to
cash it at Safeway Supermarket. So of
course they called her and, boy, did I get a
whipping for that. Charlie asked me, "What
were you thinking? Why would you do
something like that?" My response was
always "I don't know." He would always
say he wished he could spend just one day in

my head, just to see what I was thinking.
Even though I had just got into trouble for
writing a hot check, I went to school that
next week and stole twenty dollars out of a
kid's purse in the gym. Then I went to the
cafeteria and tried to by ice cream for me
and my friends. The cafeteria lady asked me
if my mom knew I was spending all my
money to buy ice cream, and when I told her
yes, she decided to call her and make sure.
Janetta was livid because she knew she
hadn't given me the money, and when she
came up there to get me, that's when she

found out I was flunking and I'd been

forging my progress reports. We sat on the

steps of Carver and she asked me why I kept

doing these things, but I couldn't even begin

to put into words how I was feeling inside.

## Abandoned...Again

So back in the system I went. Next stop: The Laura Dester Center, in Tulsa. I wasn't there long before I was sent to my first foster home in Inola, Oklahoma.

Nothing new there, really. I had been in strangers' homes before. My only thoughts were "Now how are these people going to hurt me?" I got there late in the evening. My new foster mother was Georgia Mae Roberson, an older woman but still quite spry.

I think God put her on this earth just for me, because I believe my time in Inola stopped me from making choices that were worse than those I already had up to that time.

I had a serious issue with being made to feel like all control had been taken from me, especially when it came to my free will to choose, even when those choices turned out to not be in my best interest.

Georgia Mae was a beautiful, statuesque woman with long, black, wavy hair with a streak of gray right down the middle. You could tell Indian ran through her blood. She lived on about five acres of land in a mobile home with her husband and granddaughter.

The first night I was there, she introduced me to her daughters, who were married, with children of their own, and both lived a stone's throw away. Linda was the first to make an appearance. She told me I was not to be giving her mother any flack. I was to listen, mind, and behave myself. Madeline was the second to show up, and she brought her two kids with her, Kendle and Wesley. Kendle was a lot younger than me. Wesley was closer to my age. While the adults

talked, we played hide-and-go-seek until it

was time for them to go home. Maybe this

foster home wouldn't be so bad. I really

liked Wesley. While we played he kissed me

(instant puppy love). I got settled in, and the

next day Momma Georgia went to enroll me

at Inola Elementary. Did I tell you it was a

small town? Two schools (the elementary

school kindergarten through sixth and the

high school seventh through twelfth), a little

grocery store, a gas station, and not much

else. School had already been in session for

a few months, and since most of these kids

had known each other all their lives, I just

knew I wasn't going to make any friends,

especially since it was a predominantly

white school. Well, let me put it this way:

Kendle and I were the only nonwhite people

there. Imagine my surprise when they were

actually nice to me. Nobody was trying to

beat up on me or chase me home. Some of

the first ones to befriend me were Christie

Jo, Pam, Shannon and Gaylene, and they

were some of the most popular kids in the

school it seemed. That didn't stop me from

acting up, though. I talked *all* the time. I cut

up. I made loud and weird noises in class

because it made my classmates laugh. I was

now the class clown. The teacher kept

moving me. I should have told her it was

useless; no matter where she moved me, I

was going to talk. I was always in trouble at

school for something or other. My

punishment was writing sentences, like

thousands of them. One weekend Momma

Georgia's other daughter, Erma Jean, came

to visit, and she brought along her two kids,

Brandon and Shameka. Shameka and I hit it

off right away. Finally, I had a friend whom I could share all my secrets with, somebody who could understand where I was coming from. She got me and accepted me, flaws and all. From then until now, she has been one of the constant and shining lights in my life.

Momma Georgia was a churchgoing woman. She was a member of Unity Temple Church of God in Christ, where Willie T. Cotton was the pastor. It was a small church, but I loved it. The people there were very welcoming to me. (To this day they call me family.)

I wish I could say that, because they were so nice to me, everything was peachy keen and jelly beans, but the Lord knows I was a handful and didn't always make it easy for them to love me. I'll never forget the time we were at church during a Sunday-school review and Georgia Mae told me to stop leaning on my shoes. I figured since we were in church, I was safe. So I rolled my eyes at her—what a mistake!

When the review was over and we headed

back to the Sunday-school class, Georgia

Mae confronted me about rolling my eyes at

her, and while I don't recall my exact words,

I'm pretty sure my mouth said something

smart and disrespectful. You know that

sound a switch makes in the air when it's

going real fast in the hands of a black

woman disciplining an unruly child? Well,

that's the only thing that could be heard as I

literally crawled over the other kids on the

bench in an attempt to escape her wrath. The

other children teased me about that for
months.

It seemed like we were in church all the
time. Although the congregation was few in
number, they were mighty in God. It didn't
matter if there was school the next day and
you had homework, you'd do it while
praising God. If you got sleepy, you would
go to the back pew and go to sleep. God
always came first. But it was great—they
tarried and praised God until I would
imagine the Holy Ghost saying, *"Good
Lord, people, go home; I'm tired!"* I'm just

kidding, but church mothers stayed on the altar with you until your breakthrough came.

There was an old deacon who used to sit in the front. I can't remember his name, but he would shout and praise God in that corner all by himself in his cowboy boots and hat. But even the holiest-looking people can hide bad intentions, because one summer, during vacation Bible school, I went in to get a drink of water and he cornered me in the church and kissed me. The thought of that still makes me throw up in my mouth a little bit.

Momma Georgia would sing "Jordan River," and Pastor would beat that tambourine until the bangles came off and, boy, would he preach! Holiness or hell.

We had testimony service that was cool, even though it seemed like everybody sang a song before they testified. Some would say, "Giving honor to God, who is the head of my life…" You know the rest. Those were the days. We use to play brother and sister king of the chair and Bible drill. We made sure we studied our Bible, because we wanted to make sure we stayed in that chair.

We had Young People Willing Worker; it was great. Takes me back to that old-time religion. We used to have our vacation Bible school in an old school bus in the field. I got baptized in Inola, in Pastor Cottons pond, in front of God, man, and the cows. I loved living there. I believe my love of church came from there.

For two years I lived the life. There wasn't a lot of money, but there was a lot of love, and my spirit was being fed. This might sound strange, but hear me out and maybe by the end of my story you'll understand. God

87

saved my soul, but Inola and Unity Temple
saved my life.

I had people with a direct line to God
praying for me, and although they probably
didn't understand my plight back then, in the
years to come I would need every one of
those prayers. If I had never been placed in
Momma Georgia's home, I can guarantee
you I wouldn't be here now telling my story.
I would be dead, either by my own hand or
someone else's. Isn't God amazing! I wish I
could put into words what they meant to me
over the last thirty years. After I had been

there for just over two years, my caseworker
came and delivered yet another blow: she
told me I had to leave because of abuse
allegations. I tried to tell her how untrue
those allegations were, but no one was
listening. They took me away from the very
people who had started to help me heal. Two
years of progress gone. At that moment
when I realized I could never go back to
Inola, I just knew I would never be safe
again and that anything good that happened
to me wouldn't last.

So right then, right there, I decided that if I couldn't go home, then I would do whatever I wanted to do. I wouldn't listen to anybody, because nobody ever listened to me. I didn't realize I was at one of the many crossroads I would have in my life and how much of an impact on my future the decisions I would make at that time would have. I felt so alone because everything I knew and loved was being ripped from me once again. I chose the path of self-destruction.

## Abnegation

Being thirteen years old is already difficult for most teenagers, but add in hurt, abandonment, and anger, along with having no one to guide you, and voilà! You have a dangerous combination. While I was in the shelter for that month or two, I had to go to school, and it was not an enjoyable experience. I was starting all over *again*.

I remember thinking over the years sometimes that I wished I had never gone to Inola, because, as the saying goes, you don't

miss what you never had. Even though the
Laura Dester Center was supposed to be a
temporary place, just until a home was
found for you, that wasn't always the case.
Little children got placed quickly, but with
the older children, it took a little more time.
People just didn't want to deal with the
issues that seemed to run hand in hand with
us. But the people who worked at the
shelter, you could tell most of them loved
their jobs. There was Rita. She was an
elderly lady with pure-white hair. She
walked with a cane, and if you got out of

line with her, she'd rap you across the shins
with it. There was Dot. She did not play. She
could freeze you with just one of her glares.
There were two Brenda's. One worked in
the kitchen, and the other worked with the
kids. We were always nice to the kitchen
Brenda—you know, with her handling your
food and everything. We didn't want to
wake up spewing from both ends. There was
Karen She had the longest hair, it seemed to
go on forever. She spent most of her time at
the little house where they kept the babies,
but sometimes she would come up to the

main building and spend time with us and

try to get us to believe that we were worth

something. Then there was Shaundra. She

was amazing. She was our activities

director, but so much more. Well, to me

anyway. She was always trying to encourage

me, trying to tell me I could be anything I

wanted to be. She fussed at me like I was

hers, like she really cared. I never let her

know, but I held her words close to my

heart. My time in the shelter was interesting.

I remember once there were about fifteen

kids in the shelter, girls and boys, and I got

them all to go AWOL with me. We went

around the neighborhood playing ding dong

ditch, and when we came back hours later,

the staff was not happy. I remember

Shaundra telling me I should use my power

for good. She was always trying to guide me

on the right path. I guess that was the mother

in her. Even though she had twin daughters

of her own, she always had enough love and

affection to give to us, whether we wanted it

or not.

I started eighth grade at Wilson Middle

School. I have to say that my time there was

a blur because I didn't stay there for long. I did my work and kept my head down. They found me a foster home on the north side of Tulsa.

When my caseworker took me to the home, my first thoughts were, "This is a joke, right?" They lived in what you would call a shoe-box house (because it was shaped like a shoe box). My foster mother seemed nice enough, and so did her kids. She had two daughters. One was a senior at McLain High School, but the other one, Gail, was the same age as me, so of course we were in the same grade, and I was sure we would be instant friends. Was I ever wrong.

The first thing she said to me after my caseworker left was "I don't want you here, and don't touch my stuff!" She also made sure I knew she didn't want me to sleep in her room.

I wanted to tell her how much I didn't want to be there any more than she wanted me there. While living there, I ended up going to Gilcrease Middle School. I had to ride the city bus to school because there wasn't a school bus. I thought I could go to school, keep my head down, and just ride out my time.

Well, that wasn't going to happen. Gail made sure that she told everybody she knew how I was an unwanted guest in her home and that the only reason I was there was because her mother was getting paid. I'm pretty sure Gail's mother meant me no real harm, but she tended to make a difference between me and the rest of the kids. I don't think they really understood how that can make a person feel. I already felt out of place. Her kids could go to the store, go to the park, go to the library, but I couldn't go out the front yard. Gail never let me forget I was the intruder.

Lord knows that I do believe I came to hate her and wished on numerous occasions that I could smother her in her sleep. I could not get a moment's peace.

Whatever happened at home, everybody knew it at school. Once I was sick (twenty-four-hour stomach bug) and she went and told everybody I was pregnant. Hell, I wasn't even having sex! Things finally came to a head in the worst way.

They had a talent show at school, and I wanted to be a part of it so badly that while everyone was dancing and singing I figured I'd recite a poem I had written. Big, huge mistake. I got laughed off the stage. I was so embarrassed. I tried to get away from everybody, but wouldn't you know it, I missed the city bus that I normally rode, so I ended up on the bus with Gail and some of her friends.

I went and sat all the way in the back to try to avoid contact and confrontation, yet they followed me, teasing me and calling me a crybaby.

You know a person can only take so much teasing, and after all the crap Gail had been doing to me over the past months, I had had enough! So in no uncertain terms I told her where she could go. She grabbed my things and threw them on the floor of the bus. That did it, sent me over the edge. The next thing I knew, we were on the floor of the bus fighting. It was a good thing I ended up on top because she was a big girl and could fight, and it didn't hurt that she was basically stuck in between the seats. So I got plenty of hits in before the bus stopped.

I jumped off of her and ran off the bus. I walked until I could get on another bus, which took me to a local grocery store called Best Yet. Not only did we get groceries at this store, but if need be, you could get a brand-new pair of shoes—Pro Wings, to be exact. After a while I called my caseworker, Andrea Van Dyke, and told her to come and get me.

Apparently, my foster mother had already called her, because Andrea immediately started drilling me about the fight on the bus. I tried to defend myself and gave her my side of the story, but she only gave me the speech about there being no excuse for such behavior. Then she told me that I needed to go back. I said, "Hell no!" She seemed to believe she was giving a best-case scenario by stating that it was Friday and that nothing could be done about a new place over the weekend.

I was insistent that I could not return and was willing to sleep outside before I would go back there. She advised me that my only alternative to returning was going to a local shelter and that the police would have to come pick me up and take me.

I was totally fine with that outcome and sat on the curb for about an hour before they finally came and picked me up. That foster home was a crash and burn.

## Round Two and Three and...

Back to the Laura Dester Center I went. The staff was disappointed that I hadn't been able to make the foster home work. I wasn't back at the shelter long enough to start any trouble. I wish I could tell you about the next foster home I was in, but my time there was so short; all I remember about it was that it was in Gilcrease Hills and that they never let me forget that, as far as they were concerned, I was a charity case. Oh, and I burned a patch of my hair out trying to curl it with a curling iron. I lasted about three weeks before they told Andrea to come get me. Back to the shelter I went again. This time I was in a little longer—long enough to cause all kinds of problems.

For instance, some of the boys who were in the shelter at the time were going around busting out the windows. The windows were made of Plexiglas, so they were really just cracking them, but of course I wanted to show them that I was just as tough as they were, so I decided to do it too. They didn't believe I would do it, so of course I had to show them. I went into one of the rooms with them egging me on. Shaundra and Joe

(who was the security guard at the time)

came to see what all the ruckus was about.

They walked into the room just as I cocked

my hand back to punch, and punch I did.

Only the window I decided to hit wasn't

Plexiglas. It was *glass* glass.

See, no problem. It was a perfect hole—until

I drew my arm out and the glass cut into it

down to the white meat. I didn't feel any

pain, though, until one of the girls started

screaming. I looked down, and there was

blood everywhere, and meat was just

107

hanging off my arm. She was screaming
bloody murder, so I started screaming
bloody murder, Shaundra and Joe were
screaming at me to let them see. It was a
mess. Finally, Joe grabbed a towel, grabbed
me, wrapped the towel around my arm, and
rushed me to the hospital (my hero), where
they proceeded to give me thirty-six stitches.
They said it could have been worse, that I
could have cut an artery and bled to death or
cut a nerve and permanently lost use of my
arm. After they fixed me up and sent me
back, Joe of course asked me what I'd been

108

thinking. I told him I hadn't been. He was so disappointed in me, and I hated when he gave me that look. It made me feel so guilty. I was crazy about Joe. He made me feel safe. He never looked at me or touched me in a way that made me feel uncomfortable, like some men did. So I never wanted him disappointed in me. Of course I got put on restriction, (They took all my books. I couldn't read for two weeks) and the staff was mad at me, but to the rest of the kids, I was a badass. By the time my armed healed, Andrea had found me a new foster home

My next foster home was in south Tulsa,
and my new "mom's" name was A. J. It
started out OK except with her two
grandchildren and her daughter, who lived
there. They could be such brats at times.
While there, I attended Byrd Middle School.
I didn't really have any friends or anyone to
talk to. That all changed when Keisha got to
my foster home. She was as crazy as a
Betsey bug.

Every day about the same time, she would
throw an all-out fit. I'm talking screaming,
tearing-covers-off-the-bed, rolling-on-the-

floor, and pulling-your-hair-out fit. It would

last for about thirty minutes, and then she

would just stop. I thought it was funny. She

was my sole entertainment. (I'm pretty sure

finding comfort in someone else's misery

was abnormal behavior.) After having us for

a few months, A. J. moved into a bigger

place, a house with more room and a yard.

Her daughter had left with the kids, so it was

just me and Keisha, but then LaShell

arrived, and I just have to tell you: a house

full of women is not fun at all. We bumped

heads from the get-go. I figured that since I

111

was the first one there, I was the boss. Why

not? That did not go very well with LaShell.

She figured that since she was the oldest,

she was the boss—a month older. *Please.*

Well, since we were the only company we

had, we did what anybody would do when

locked up together: we tortured each other.

The first one who went to sleep got it the

worst. We would put shaving cream in her

hands and toothpaste in her mouth if she

slept with her mouth open. We even put

soap in a sock and would beat each other

with it.

But I have to admit that the cruelest thing was when Shell told Keisha that when she started her period, she was going to die. You see, Keisha wasn't all the way tight up there in the mind, so you can only imagine what happened the day her monthly friend showed up.

I have to admit that over twenty years later, I still get a good laugh every time I think about when Keisha went into the bathroom that day and came out screaming bloody murder—no pun intended—with her classic Diana Ross–looking eyes and her hands

113

covered in what she called death. We laughed so hard. Anyway, I finished my eighth-grade year there and started my ninth-grade year at Memorial High School, and that's when the real problems started.

I began feeling like a prisoner in my foster home. We couldn't go anywhere, couldn't receive or make phone calls, and weren't allowed to go to school functions. Not only did we have to clean the house from top to bottom (while A. J.'s grandkids made a mess), we also had to go to work with her and clean other people's homes too. This

114

concerned me because she got about $500 a month for each of us, and we didn't see any of it. She also received clothing vouchers, so it wasn't like she had to use her "paycheck" for clothes. We didn't even get to pick out our own clothes. I felt like I was trapped, so I started skipping school and hanging with my friends. It wasn't long before my grades started to drop.

I ended up in the dean's office too many times to count. Well, on this one particular day, everything just went totally crazy. I can remember it like it was yesterday. I had on a mini blue-jean skirt; a sleeveless, button-down shirt; and some white Keds. Shell, Mabel (one of the girls from school), and I were skipping class during the second lunch period. We were in the annex bathroom playing around when a couple of guys who had classes with us, and who were also cutting class, started playing around as well.

Pretty soon we had locked ourselves in the stalls, and they were trying to get in. We were laughing and screaming so loud that some of the teachers came to investigate. We were being escorted by three teachers and the security guard to the dean's office.

The dean told us that she was finally going

to get us out of her school, because our kind

was trouble. I think the devil got right into

me at the moment, because I told her to fuck

herself and that she and that school could go

straight to hell, and then I turned around and

walked right out of the office.

I remember the security guard followed me

around, and I told him that he couldn't catch

me if I didn't want him to. So to prove it, I

took off running. Now, remember it was still

the lunch period, so it was loud and noisy. I

117

have to tell you I really must have lost my mind that day, because I went to the pay phone in the cafeteria (this was before cell phones), and I called the police. I told them I was a school official and said that we were having a riot and that we needed the police. With all the background noise, you would have believed me too.

I went into the cafeteria, sat down, and ate some lunch. Now, about thirty minutes later, as I was walking the halls, Shell and a boy from my English class ran up to me and told me that the police were there and they were

118

looking for me. Shell was jumping all around me, asking, "What are you going to do? What are you going to do?" Then my classmate told me that I could hide at his house. Yeah, *right!*

I had no brilliant plan of my own, and the only thing that made sense at the moment was to run. And run I did—smack dab into a police officer. I mean, literally bounced off of him. He tried to grab me, but I turned around and hauled ass. I was running across the parking lot with this cop chasing me. Then I saw two more ahead of me, so I turned and ran back into the school, laughing the entire time. Have you ever tried to run and laugh at the same time?

I was running down the hall, and out of nowhere someone pushed me into this room. The first thing I remember was smelling cigarette smoke. I saw a door at the back of the room I had been pushed into, so I went to investigate and thrust myself through the door. It was just my luck: I was in the teachers' lounge. So I walked back into the main room just in time to see the security guard crack the door open and put two fire extinguishers inside. I remember thinking, "What the hell!"

The next thing I know, two big, burly cops walk into the room. The first one says, "Sit down!"

So of course I just had to say, "Make me." As he approached to grab me, I started swinging.

Apparently I had forgotten about the other cop. He grabbed me. I started turning and twisting and kicking. Doing whatever it took to get away from them. Did I mention that I had on a skirt? One of the cops grabbed me, and he put my head between his legs, and when he did, I bit him on the thigh really hard, so hard, in fact, that his response was to hit me in the head with his flashlight. It took about thirty minutes and one more person before they got me handcuffed.

Later they told the judge that I must have been on drugs because it shouldn't have taken three grown men to restrain a fourteen-year-old girl. They took me into custody and charged me with first-degree arson. First-degree arson? Really? They said

I had tried to set the school on fire. (With what, my breath?) There were no matches to be found, no evidence of the sort. Just their word against mine, although I have to admit my word didn't hold much water after the show I had put on.

So this was my first trip into juvenile detention (but far from my last), and it was horrible. First, they take everything you have from you. Then they make you take a bath and wash your hair with this god-awful soap, and on top of that, they watch you while you shower. I was not a happy camper. They made me wear juvie-issue

clothing from the skin out. I tried really hard

not to think about who had on that

underwear before me.

Then they put you into the general

population, which at this particular facility

meant boys and girls were mingled together.

Wherever we were, we were locked in

together. When it was time to eat, they took

us into the cafeteria, counted out the

silverware, and fed us. When we were done

with our fine dining, we had to sit there to

make sure they got back the same amount of silverware.

During the week, they had this little school that we would attend. It was too small for my taste, and I sure would have hated for there to be a fire. We went outside once a day. That was the best time.

I remember we played dodgeball a lot. You know, now that I think about it, was that really the best game for a bunch of angry and dangerous kids to play? Anyway, I was in there for two months—two months of playing cards and dominoes. At least at the shelter they taught me to play chess. My public defender kept trying to get me to plead guilty to first-degree arson, but I adamantly refused.

I told him I wasn't pleading guilty to something I didn't do. So the judge told me I would stay there until I admitted it or told who did it. Being in rare form, I addressed the judge, saying, "Excuse me, Judge, but don't you think that if somebody actually tried to set the school on fire, there would

have been some kind of evidence? Duh! Do
I look like an idiot?"

Needless to say, that judge didn't realize that
stubborn was my middle name. They
dropped the charges to disturbing the peace.
I'll take that one. So I got out and went back
to A. J., but they had me on this system
where I had to be in the house at a certain
time, and if I left the house, I had to call this
number and report it.

I think the person who was the most
embarrassed by this ordeal was my cousin

Boobie, because she had graduated from Memorial, and everybody knew we were related. Oh well, sorry, Cousin.

After that I couldn't go back to school, and A. J. didn't want me in her house by myself. She was always saying little things on the sly to me, and she let her *grown* kids talk to myself, LaShell and Keisha crazy and treat us horribly. You can only take crap like that for so long, so I decided in my mind, "Why would I stay somewhere and let somebody get paid to mistreat me?" I don't think so! We were her extra money. By this time there

128

were four of us: Keisha, Shell, Gladys, and me.

So being the self-professed leader of the pack, I convinced everybody to run away with me. It was so funny and, amazingly, so very easy. We just waited for A. J. to go to bed. She always locked herself in her bedroom as if we were going to murder her in her sleep or something. When we were sure she was asleep, we let up the garage door and walked out. Simple.

Shell was the one with a boyfriend, so we went to his house and spent the night, and the next morning we called my social worker. You can imagine she was not a happy, but she hid it well. I don't think her own kids gave her as many problems as I did, but she always hung in there, and she never gave up on me.

So it was back to the shelter for us, and when they saw us walking through the door, all they could do was laugh. That probably wasn't the right reaction, but, hey, what can I say? Now, I thought LaShell and Keisha had my back, but after about three days in the shelter, they weaseled out and decided to ask if they could go back.

Not me, though. I had entirely too much ego to do that, and pretty soon they left me there and went back to the foster home. I'll admit I was sad to see them go. About two weeks later, I went AWOL and went to see Shell at school. When I got there, I sneaked into the school and went to her class. We skipped school for the rest of the day and just hung out. Now, getting to Memorial High School wasn't that bad; I caught the bus. But getting back was a whole different story, because I didn't have any bus fare to get back, and—wouldn't you know—nobody else had any money either. So I decided to just walk back. Really, how bad could it be? So when school was out for the day, I started heading back to the Laura Dester Center. Oh my God, that was a long walk! I swear it took me every bit of six hours to make that walk. My feet were numb by the time I got to where I was going, and wouldn't you know that right when I was around the corner from the shelter, some fool stopped to offer me a ride. If my feet hadn't been in so much pain,

I probably would have cussed him out, but

after that walk, who had the energy? I think

it took me a good month to recover.

## My First Group Home

Now, as I said before, Andrea was a great
social worker. But I have to say, this next
placement made me wonder. I don't know
why she thought I'd be a good fit for this
next placement she found for me. It was
called the Francis E. Willard, right down the
street from the Gilcrease Museum, in Tulsa.

Before I could get in, there were numerous
things I had to do. I was required to be on
birth control. At first I didn't see the point,
because there were no boys around. And in
order to be put on birth control, I had to

have a complete physical. (Can you say, "first pap smear"?) Oh My God! And to make matters worse, the one to perform it was a young, black, cute male doctor. I was very disturbed that some strange man was looking at my hoo-hah. It brought back all kind of memories

You would think that as a young girl, I would have been given a female doctor, but, hey, who am I to say? Finally, after all that they let me in, and from what I remember, it was a nice-looking place. It was very large and had a main house that you passed as you

135

drove through the gates, along with six

cottages. The grounds were immaculate,

with multiple huge gardens and an awesome

pool. I was in the Lyons Cottage, and there

were about six or seven girls to each cottage.

I thought, "Wow, this is going to be so

cool." Yeah, *right!*

So the first thing they do is let you meet all

the girls on the property. Then you go back

to your cottage and go over the rules of your

new home. There was a wonderful kitchen,

an exercise room, and a great big family

room, and on the upper floors were the bedrooms. It was very nice.

I didn't find out until later, but Andrea had managed to pull some strings to get me in. It wasn't a state-run facility, which means I was the only foster kid in the whole place. All the other girls who were there came from affluent homes, and they were there for myriad reasons, from multiple suicide attempts to just plain bad behavior.

Anyway, the first set of rules we went over were the kitchen rules, and, first and foremost, everyone helped with the meals.

Every week we would sit down as a group

and plan the menu, and every day everyone

helped prepare the meals, which was fine

with me; after the meal was prepared, we

would all sit down and eat together. Here

comes the kicker, though. As a young

person, I was always told, "If you don't like

something, don't put it on your plate," but

here things were totally different. It didn't

matter whether you liked something or not;

if it was on the menu, you had to eat it, and

if you didn't eat it, you got points and points

weren't a good thing. I can't tell you how many points I got over food.

Once we went on a picnic, and they brought cucumber sandwiches! Who the heck eats cucumber sandwiches? Not this girl, so guess what—points. Now, you might be thinking that points shouldn't be that big a deal, but just wait. Points had everything to do with everything.

I was assigned chores. Some were inside chores, and others were outdoor chores. That glorious landscaping that I spoke about earlier? Well, you guessed it: no one was paid to do it; we did it all. If your chores weren't done right, you got points.

The point system ruled our existence at Willard. It dictated what level you were on, which dictated what you could do. You had to be on the right level to go off the premises; you had to be on the right level to be in your room for reasons other than sleep; you had to be on the right level to watch TV; and you had to be on the right level even to use the phone. Needless to say, I was never on the right level. I even got in trouble for

not participating in group-therapy sessions.

But who can really blame me? They sat you

in what they called the "hot seat" and then

started asking you all these stupid questions

or telling you why you felt the way you felt.

I remember thinking toward my peers,

"Y'all know nothing about me, with your

rich parents and nice homes. You couldn't

even begin to understand the shoes I have to

walk in."

So every session I just looked at them and never said one word. For three months I never talked in the group sessions.

God knows I hated that place, and everything about it just seemed wrong. Nothing abusive, really, just crazy stuff. I picked weeds out of the garden, cultivated the trees and plants, planted seeds, raked, and mowed.

Now, being the only black person there, I kind of felt like I was on the plantation, and when one of the girls got mad at me and

called me a nigger, I knew it. So of course
my temper being as hair-trigger as it was, I
picked up one of those garden claws and
threatened to poke out her eyes and cut out
her tongue, and of course I got in trouble.
No one wanted an explanation about why I
had done what I did. All that mattered was
that I had threatened someone. So they gave
me extra chores outside and wouldn't let me
call Andrea.

My response was to kick a hole in the wall,
and I took off walking. It was one hundred
degrees outside, but I wasn't staying in that

place one more day! I didn't even take anything with me. It was about eight thirty in the morning when I walked off the grounds and kept walking.

It was about five hours later before I made it to my first stop: Cousin Vanessa's place, on Main Street. Whew! Was I hot and hungry by the time I arrived! Of course, everybody tried to get me to eat, but in my mind that made me feel like I was begging, so I said I wasn't hungry.

After resting up and visiting with them for a while, I continued my journey. It was a Friday and was now creeping up on 5:00 p.m., so the CPS office was closed for the weekend, and I didn't have a way to get in contact with Andrea. Even knowing that the shelter workers might not let me in, I walked right up to the shelter door and rang the bell and told them I was there to check myself in.

The looks on the workers' faces was priceless, but they let me in.

**The First Time**

After I left Francis Willard, things weren't
the greatest. There weren't many foster
homes for kids my age, so I stayed at the
shelter for a while.

To break the boredom, I tended to go
AWOL. I figured that since all I had to do to
get back in is ring the doorbell, then why
not? I'd be lying if I said that all the workers
at the shelter liked me, because there was
one who couldn't stand me, but rest assured
the feeling was mutual. Tony was one of the

146

biggest assholes I had ever met (in my

opinion). I had gone AWOL, and I rang the

doorbell, and Tony answered, but he

wouldn't let me in. He said if I wanted to get

back in, then I would have to have the police

bring me. He said he was tired of my

thinking I could come and go as I pleased,

and then he closed the door in my face.

Well, I wasn't going to beg for him to let me

in, so I just turned around and started

walking.

I walked around downtown, and Mayfest was going on, so I saw plenty of people whom I knew, but the later it got, the more people started going home, until it was just me and this boy I had gone to school with. We started walking and talking. (Nobody knew I was in the shelter. I guess they thought I had parents who didn't care what I did.)

So anyway, he asked me if I wanted to go to his house, because his mom worked nights. It was cold out and I didn't have anywhere else to go, so I went.

148

## Some Hurts Are Beyond Tears

It was kind of awkward. I knew what he wanted, but I needed a place to stay warm. So I figured fair exchange—no robbery. I could do this—just lay there and not think about it.

I guess I should feel bad about trading sex for a warm place to stay, but I just couldn't make myself feel bad. The next morning, I went to my caseworker's office so she could take me back to the shelter.

As I sat there waiting for her to take me back, I wondered why I felt so numb on the inside. I felt way older than my fourteen years. What I had done the night before should have made me feel so dirty. I guess when you feel dirty all the time, what's a little more. Being in the shelter was comfortable for me. The staff for the most part really liked their jobs and working with us, even though you found those few who were in it for the wrong reasons (they didn't last long). As for the kids who came through the shelter, some you couldn't stand and some you bonded with due to circumstances.

I had a problem letting people get to close to me. I always felt that if you cared too much, if you loved too much, that person had the power to destroy your heart, and I hardly had any pieces left. But I did find two girls with whom, for a season, I was best of friends.

All my life I've heard the saying "God looks out for old folks, children, and fools." Well, two of those I had down to a T. (I'll let you decide which.)

I had two really good friends, Amy and Rachel. They would've stormed the gates of hell with just a bucket of water if I had asked them to. They were some ride-or-die friends.

Amy was a little white girl with big blue eyes and blond hair cut real short. She kind of looked like a pixie—that is, until she opened her mouth. Then she sounded blacker than I did. Rachel, on the other hand, was the exact opposite.

## Some Hurts Are Beyond Tears

She was a little, quiet, shy, brunette
Hispanic, and out of us all, she was the most
fragile one, the one we protected. No one
messed with Rachel, or they would have me
to deal with. Well, back in the day they used
to have this place called the Fontana out in
southern Tulsa where you could get into the
movies for one dollar, and it was the place
where everybody who was anybody our age
hung out, so of course we had to be there.

Most everyone hung out in the parking lot.
You know, I'm still racking my brain about

153

how we used to get there, but, hey, we were in the spot!

One day Rachel, Amy, and I ran away. We were just chillin', walking around town until Amy said, "Hey, let's go to the movies." Rachel and I agreed and asked Amy about where to see the movie. Just then I got a bright idea and suggested we go to California. And of course those idiots said yes. Boy, were we a mess!

You see, I wanted to go to California because that's where my family was—my daddy, grandmother, aunts, and uncles. I always thought that maybe they just didn't know where I was and if I could just get to them, they would let me live with them and everything would be OK. Now, back then we were fourteen years of age, but we looked a lot older, or so we were told. If guys asked us how old we were, we would tell them we were seventeen. But I've seen some pictures of me at fourteen years, and I have to say I don't know what they were seeing, but I didn't look anywhere near that age.

We figured if we just started heading west, we would get to California one way or another. So we got on the freeway and just started walking. We were singing and laughing and just having a great time. So the first people to stop were these two older white guys in a station wagon. Would you believe they were wrestling promoters? They took us all the way into Okmulgee (about 40 minutes from Tulsa) and dropped us off. We were walking around looking lost, and it was getting late in the day when this old, black man in this beat-up pickup truck stopped and asked us where we were heading.

Now, mind you, we had come up with this big, elaborate story about how my mom was sick and on her deathbed in California and I was trying to get to her. Oh, did I mention we were crazy? We had to be: a black girl (me), a white girl who thought she was black (Amy), and a mixed Hispanic chick (Rachel).

We were all so different but closer than some real sisters. I was a fighter. Rachel was so sweet and quiet (I still don't know what she was doing hanging with us) and Amy, well if we didn't want to do something, Amy would…I'll let you use your own imagination.

As I was saying, this old man stopped, and when I say old, I mean old. His wrinkles had wrinkles. He asked us where we were going, and we gave him our story, and he said, "You girls don't need to be out here. Come with me, and I'll get my nephew to take you all to Oklahoma City." Can someone say,

"Side of a milk carton: 'Have you seen me'?"

So of course we hopped in the truck with our silly butts and said OK. He took us all the way out in the sticks to this little shack-like house (real old school) and called his nephew. About thirty minutes later, this Cadillac arrived and out step three men, and I use that term very loosely.

They were about twenty, I think. So the old man told them our dilemma and one of them said, "Sure, we'll take them." And of course we went with them.

We thought it was fun and exciting. Did I mention that we had the nerve to *pray* before we left Tulsa? Dimples was the name of the one driving the Caddy. He had a wet Jheri curl and gold in his mouth, and he made a beeline for Amy. Then there was Boadee. He had a fancy for yours truly. I can't remember the name of the third man, but he hooked up with Rachel. They wanted to show us a good time, so they bought drinks

160

and introduced us to weed (a.k.a. marijuana).

We thought we were the shit. I think we wasted more of their weed than smoked it, because we didn't know how to inhale. We stayed with them for about two days, and then they started talking about keeping us.

They told us we didn't have to leave, that we could cook and clean for them and that they would take care of us and we could live with them and not worry about anything. This was quite creepy, to say the least.

So we waited until they got really drunk and passed out, and then we took their keys and threw them outside in the bushes. I said we should take all their money, but Rachel said they were already going to be mad, so we shouldn't do anything that would make them chase us down and kill us. So I only took ten dollars.

It was about 1:00 a.m. when we started walking, and it seemed like we walked forever, and it just happened to be very nippy that night. We finally came to a Denny's and ordered this big plate of french fries and drinks. There went the ten dollars. I bet they wished they would have let me take all the money after all. The waitress started asking us too many questions, so we left.

Wouldn't you know she called the police, because no sooner had we made it back on the highway than here come the police with their lights flashing. After five days of being on the run, we had only made it to El Reno, Oklahoma. It doesn't even take five days to get to California, and yet we hadn't even made it out the state of Oklahoma!

The police took us to the El Reno Youth Shelter, where they questioned us; we confessed to running away from the shelter in Tulsa.

After our interrogation they let us take showers and gave us fresh clothes to wear the next day. We got dressed and ran out of the shelter laughing because we had gotten away, or so we thought.

Not ten minutes into our "escape," we were walking past a park when, all of a sudden, three police cars came tearing around the corner with their lights flashing and sirens blaring. We took off running, and they jumped out of their vehicles and started chasing us as if we had stolen something.

Unfortunately, we weren't fast enough. We ran into the park and hid behind this old, dead tree that had fallen over.

The cars screeched into the park, and the police jumped out with their guns and flashlights drawn. (You'd think we were some hardened criminals the way they were acting.) They caught us, handcuffed us, and

took us back to the shelter, and this time
they were smart enough to separate us for
the night and when they transported us back
to Tulsa.

When we got back to the shelter, we
showered and ate, but they took our shoes,
thinking that nobody runs away barefoot
when the seasons are changing. Well, almost
nobody, because that's exactly what Amy
did. She begged me and Rachel to come
with her, but we were cold and tired.

We begged Amy to stay. We'd rest up and wait until it got warmer. Rachel and I tried to talk her out of it, but she didn't listen. That's the last time I ever saw or heard about her. I always thought that maybe she got killed or something, but I sure hope I'm wrong about that.

The thing about it is, once you become a ward of the court and get into the system, somebody somewhere has heard something. Your caseworker, maybe a foster parent whom you might keep in touch with, or a friend—anybody. But not Amy. It was as if she disappeared off the face of the earth.

After a while, with not many foster homes available for kids our age and all the emotional baggage we were dealing with, they put Rachel in the psych ward, drugged her up on all kinds of stuff until she didn't come out the same.

Now me—I never stayed still long enough for them to admit me. Besides, as I mentioned before, I had a *great* social worker, and she came up with all kinds of creative ways to keep me out of places like that. And let's not forget that even though I didn't yet realize it, God had a plan for my life!

Amy had disappeared, and Rachel had gone to a foster home. Now all of my runaway buddies were gone. So for a few weeks, I stayed put. Then my friend LaShell came back to the shelter, and she told me about this guy she was messing with who had his own place out in west Tulsa at some apartments on Turkey Mountain, and she wanted to know if I wanted to go with her. Sure, why not.

So we ran from the shelter and headed to his house. Now, on our way there, she was telling me about all the things she had been up to since the last time we saw each other. Then she told me how she had stolen a shirt from a store and almost got caught. I was like, "Really, a shirt?" I told her I was a better thief than that.

So of course I had to prove it. So after we got to the apartment, we hung out for a few days, then she reminded me about our little

bet. So I got up to walk to the store. It took

an hour to get down that hill from the

apartment.

But I finally made it. I wanted to go to the

little store that sold the clothes, and as I

walked in, I noticed that there was only one

worker, and she was vacuuming, so I walked

in like I belonged, and she asked me if she

could help me, and I told her that I was

shopping for school clothes.

She told me OK and said to let her know if I needed any help. I responded that I would and started picking out clothes as if I were really going to buy something. After a little while, she was vacuuming again and kind of went to the back. I had all these clothes in my hand, and just as I started to walk out, somebody walked in.

I was so nervous! I was like, "OK, what to do? Glennette, what to do? Do I put it back or do I run out the store?" Yes, you guessed it: I ran out of the store, around the back, and into the alley, hoping nobody would find me. When it was all said and done, I had stolen about $300 worth of clothes. At that time I thought it was so funny and that I was doing something so big. The night after we finished counting up the value of the clothes I had taken, I grew tired of being over to that man's house and I decided to go back to the shelter—just me and my loot. So I called a cab to take me to the Fontana Center. Which got me a little closer to where I was trying to go.

So cab fare to Fontana was about sixty dollars, and of course I didn't have that, so

right before the driver was about to ask me
for it, I jumped out of the cab and started
running. As my luck would have it, I jumped
out right in front of a cop who was on a
motorcycle, just sitting there on his break.
So the next thing you know I was
surrounded by police officers. They arrested
me, put me in the car, and took me back to
the shelter. Once I was back at the shelter,
the staff took my clothes because they knew
I had stolen them.

So not only was I on restriction, but I didn't
have my new, nice clothes. I was so

bummed out, all I could do was go outside. I wasn't allowed to do any activities or participate in any outings, so I just sat there bored. Across the field from the shelter I was staying in, there was a place called Youth Services of Tulsa.

While the Laura Dester Center was a shelter that housed kids who had been adjudicated deprived (e.g., abused, abandoned, etc.), Youth Services of Tulsa housed runaways and kids who had other issues.

We all shared the same area when we would

go outside and play. Of course, we were told

not to talk to each other, so as you can

imagine, we did the opposite. And as

always, when a bunch of kids get together,

somebody has to be the boss, so this one kid

thought it would be him. Somehow or other

he and I got into it. I can't remember if he

spit on me or called me a Nigger or both, but

the fight was on. You know the dirty little

kid in *Peanuts*? Everywhere he walks

there's a mini dust storm? Well, that was us.

We were fighting so hard that all you could

176

see was a tiny dust storm. Joe came to that boy's rescue. He grabbed me up by the back of my collar and gave me a shake and told me to calm down. I was spitting mad, but of course I couldn't attack Joe. So I stood there fuming while he got to the bottom of the situation. The boy said something smart to me, so I jumped on him again. I tried to stomp a mud hole into him before Joe literally dragged me back into the shelter. Then he started fussing at me, by this time I didn't care if I disappointed him or not I was so mad! Of course they took away my outside privileges. It seemed like forever before I could go back outside (It was really only about 3 days). That's when I met Kevin and Stacy. Every time we were outside together, we sat and talked, and eventually the light conversation about the weather and sports progressed toward running away and—voila!—I had new runaway buddies.

Easter Sunday was the day we ran away. We started off walking, but before long people stopped to pick us up. From the back Kevin looked like a girl, so most people stopped because they thought it was three girls. It

took us three days before we made it to
California. As soon as we got there, they left
me. So as was my custom, I called my
caseworker.

It's a wonder Andrea didn't wash her hands
of me, but she was always so calm with me.
She called the authorities and had them pick
me up, and they took me to a Soap home.
(That's what they called foster homes in Los
Angeles.)

I was to stay there until they arranged a
flight back to Tulsa for me. They put me in a

home in El Monte, California, *where no one in the house spoke English!*

How in the world are you going to put an English-speaking person in a Spanish household where *nobody* speaks English? There was a lot of bootleg sign language used instead. I was there for two very long weeks. Finally, I was put on a nonstop flight back to Tulsa. One good thing about that experience was that I got a new wardrobe.

When I made it back, boy, did Andrea let me have it! I felt so guilty. She told me how people worry about me and how I could end

up dead or worse if I kept running away.

Lord knows I really should have listened to

her.

## My Worst Nightmare

I'd finally made it back to Tulsa, and I had a whole new wardrobe and a new attitude. I thought I was so cute. I was fourteen years old, and nobody could tell me anything.

The conversation I'd had earlier with my caseworker had totally slipped my mind. When I got back to the shelter, I found out one of my friends named Tina was there. It was the weekend, so school was out, and what did we decide to do? You guessed it: we ran away.

We caught a ride to the north side to see whom we could hang out with. We hung around there until she told me she wanted to go see some friends in Apache Manor. And I was all in. So we went to her friend's apartment, where they were having a smoke-out, getting high and drunk.

But I noticed that all the people at the party were much older than we were, and the lady who owned the apartment noticed too, because she told us we had to go and to leave immediately.

Two of Tina's friends were telling her that we were cool, but the owner didn't think we were cool enough to be in her house and send her to jail. She was so upset that she even made those who thought we were cool leave as well.

When we left, I remember it being very late, and I was so ready to go, but the guys really wanted us to stay, and Tina just wouldn't leave.

Apparently, there was more than one unit these guys frequented in the complex, and soon we were arriving at another apartment

that they spent time at. Obviously, I didn't

have the sense God gave a rat, because if I

had, I would have left her ass and took off,

but no, I walked into the apartment. My first

mistake.

Any fool could tell by the way the apartment

was set up that it wasn't anything other than

a hangout spot. So we all sat down, and they

told us they had something that would make

us feel better than we had ever felt before.

Just then one of the guys pulled this glass

tube out of his pocket, got a lighter, and started burning the whole thing.

I remember him taking a little whitish pebble out of a baggie and putting it into the pipe and it turning white with black scorch marks and thinking, "What the hell is that?"

That was not a joint, the one drug I was used to. We just sat there looking at the guys and looking at each other. *Now* she was ready to go. We began making excuses to get out of there, and they were trying to get us to hit the pipe. We were like, "Naw, that's OK.

It's late, and we really have to go." They really didn't want us to go. Then all of a sudden, Tina said she had to go to the bathroom, and one of the guys said, "That's cool. I'll show you where it is."

That heifer left me in the room with the other guy. I think his name was Eric. Mistake number two!

There I was, sitting there twiddling my fingers, waiting for her to come back. Eric comes and sits on the couch next to me, telling me that I didn't have to be nervous and that I should take a hit of the pipe because it would mellow me out.

Now, I had what you would call inhalation issues; I hadn't learned yet how to inhale stuff into my lungs. So I figured that if I just puffed on it, he might leave me alone.

So I did. Good thing I didn't inhale, because I might have been a crackhead by now if I had. That was my first run-in with crack cocaine. I was still sitting there waiting for Stacy to come back in the room when Eric exclaimed, "She ain't coming back no time soon. She's probably in there doing her thing with my boy."

Then he said to me, "Why don't you loosen up and have some fun like your friend?" At that point I was scared spitless. Nobody knew where we were, and this guy was high and was tall, broad-shouldered, and intimidating.

It was a horrible feeling—trapped with no way out. He began to kiss and touch on me, and I tried to wiggle away. I kept saying that I had to go home so I wouldn't get in

189

trouble. But he wasn't listening, and he pulled me to the floor, trying to get into my pants. I remember just trying to keep his hands off of me and telling him to stop. All the while he kept telling me that I knew what was going to happen when I came up there with him.

I told him I didn't want to do this; I just wanted to go home. He raised up off of me, and I thought it was over and I would be able to leave, but instead—and I don't even remember where he pulled it from—he pulled out this huge gun and sat it right

190

beside my head. He looked at me and asked me if I still wanted to go home.

I was so scared I couldn't say anything. This was it. I knew what was going to happen. He was going to rape me and then shoot me. I knew what he looked like; he couldn't really let me leave. I lay there as he invaded my body.

I looked at the peeling paint on the walls, the cracks in the ceiling. I couldn't even cry. This hovel would be my last sight before I died. Would it hurt to die? Would anybody

look for me? Would they even miss me?
Please, God, if you get me out of this, I'll
change, and I'll be good. I lay there while he
grunted and sweated on me. I felt helpless
and hopeless. I don't know how long it went
on. It felt like forever. The pain was
agonizing. Finally, he grunted and fell on
top of me.

I just lay there, too scared of what was
coming next to move. After a while he
started to snore.

The bastard had fallen asleep. I continued to lay there. What if he was faking? He was asleep. I tried to ease myself from underneath him, but he was so heavy. I was afraid to push too hard. What if he woke up? All of a sudden, he rolled over onto his back. He never woke up. I looked at the gun and thought how easy it would be to pick up that gun and point it at his head and pull the trigger.

Then I heard this small voice in the back of my mind say that if I picked it up and used it on myself, no one could ever hurt me again.

It would be over. No more pain. It was oh so tempting. I stood up, reached for my clothes, got dressed as fast as I could, and then ran. I lost a piece of myself that night.

I made my way back to the shelter, and they let me in. I remember Joe (head of security) asking me what was wrong, but I just couldn't bear to talk to him.

I ran up the stairs thinking that I could talk to one of the female workers; I just knew one of them would help me. I told one of them what happened, and she, surprisingly, told me it was my own fault for putting myself in that predicament. Then she said, "I bet you won't run away again." Then she turned and walked off.

I didn't tell anyone else. I was so full of rage that I fought all the time. As months went by, my temper became uncontrollable. Anything would set me off. Nobody was safe from my anger—boy, girl, man, or woman. One morning we were in the dining area eating breakfast; a girl named Nicole took my cinnamon toast, and I completely lost it. It took three grown-ups to pull me off

195

her. They said afterward I was like a pit bull locked on my prey.

I just wanted to hurt somebody else, because I was hurting so bad on the inside. They sent me to the detention center because I was being extra violent.

One of the tests they give you when admitted is a pregnancy test, and wouldn't you know it—mine showed positive. They made me stay locked out for a few weeks until the kids that I would run away with had left the shelter. While I was in the detention center, one of the workers started pushing up on me. He would make suggestive comments. He would stand to close and rub against me when nobody was watching. He would even come on the girls unit and stand in front of my door and look at me, even though he worked the boys unit. The day I left to go back to the Shelter and my belongings were given back to me. He had placed his phone number and a little note that said if I ever needed a place to stay to call him. I held on to the note for some reason. They sent me back to the shelter and when others found out that I was pregnant.

They were so disappointed in me. "How could you let this happen?" they would ask me. Yeah, like I had a choice. They never asked; they only assumed. I never said anything different.

## Will I Ever Learn?

Of course, when it was found out I was pregnant, having an abortion was discussed, and much to the dismay of some, I said no. I think I decided not to mostly because people whose opinion I never asked for always had something negative to say about me. They would constantly tell me what I needed to do, so of course I did the opposite.

Yet again, Andrea found me a place to go. She found a placement for me at a group home in Oklahoma City. I couldn't go for another few weeks, so, unfortunately, this provided plenty of time for me to cause lots of havoc.

I pushed what had happened to me to the back of my mind. I was good at disassociating myself from things that were too painful to face.

I kept putting myself in dangerous situations. I went AWOL again, this time with a young girl named Miriam. She wanted to go see her parents, who owned some type of juke joint on the north side. So we went and hung out and there for a while. After several hours, she told me she would be back and then left. I waited and waited and waited some more, until I fell asleep in one of the booths. When I woke up, Miriam had not returned from wherever she had gone. I was still waiting. You would think I would at least have the sense God gave a rat, but apparently not.

A guy who was a friend of Miriam's father came up to me and told me he knew where Miriam had gone and asked if I would like for him to give me a ride. Like a dummy, I said yes, never thinking that I might be in danger. I got in the car, and as he started driving, he told me that first he needed to go by his apartment because he had to get something.

Even though I didn't really feel comfortable, there were no "Oh my God, he's a serial killer" vibes going off, so I went along. This guy lived all the way out in eastern Tulsa. Now, by this time I started to feel very uncomfortable, and I probably should have had my pervert radar fixed. When we got to his apartment, he asked me to come up, citing how hot it was and how miserable I would be in the hot car. So I went up into his apartment and sat on the couch. Just then he locked the door behind us.

Now, instead of getting what he said he had come to get, he sat on the sofa beside me. So I jumped up and headed to the door; he started grabbing me, telling me how I knew I wanted this and how I was so going to enjoy it. So I started yelling at him to let me go, and through all my kicking and screaming, I began knocking stuff over, trying to make as much noise as I could.

203

I figured it was the middle of the day;
somebody should have been home! It
seemed like forever, but there was a knock
at the door. He went to the door and cracked
it open. There was this tiny old white
woman standing there asking if everything
was all right.

I took that opportunity and squeezed right
on by him and out the door, and then I took
off running.

I ran until I was too tired and too hot to run
anymore. I felt like I was way out in the

middle of nowhere. I didn't have anybody to call to pick me up, so I knew I was in for a long walk. I walked for what seemed like forever, which in reality was probably more like two hours at that point.

All I wanted to do was get back to the shelter. So about thirty minutes later, this car pulled up, and an older man, about fortyish, stopped and asked me if I needed a ride. Now, about this time I was desperate. I was hot, and it was getting late, so I said yes. I told him I was going to Hillcrest Medical Center. Everything was cool until we got on the highway, and all of a sudden he said,

"You know, you shouldn't get into cars with

strange men." That's when I started praying!

I was bargaining with God, saying, "Lord, if

you get me out of this, I will never ever get

into cars with people I don't know!"

Now, most people would have probably said

they would never run away again, but since

God knew I would have been lying, I

decided not to push my luck. I was already

on shaky ground with him anyway.

I told the driver that he could just stop the car and let me out. He refused and began to speed up. He told me he was going to keep me and take me to Vegas. I was in such a panic that I grabbed the door handle and told him if he didn't stop the car, I was going to jump out right then and there, and just in case he thought I was joking, I opened the door.

Now, whether I would have done it or not is something I'm glad I never had to find out, because he slowed down and pulled over. As

I was jumping out of the car, he said, "That will teach you to ride with strangers."

I finally made it back to the shelter as the sun was going down, all the while telling myself that if I learned my lesson, I would never do that again. Never say never.

## OKC Bound

They found me a group home in Oklahoma City. It wasn't much different than the other institutions I had been in. There were a bunch of girls in the house, and I was the youngest and the only one who was pregnant. I believe that because I wasn't showing that much, it all wasn't real to me yet.

The first thing they did when I got there was put me in summer school. Who in the hell wants to go to school in the Oklahoma heat?

I was not happy, and they didn't care if I was going to stay there, just as long as I followed the rules.

My caseworker impressed upon me the fact that this was my last chance. I was now at the age where no one wanted me. Who wants an emotionally stunted, angry, pregnant fifteen-year-old?

I had even conceived a year sooner than my preacher-kid mom! I don't know if I ever wanted to break the cycle or if I deliberately set out to be just like her. I only know that I was turning out be an apple that didn't fall

far—at all.

**Another Start**

My summer in the group home was
uneventful. My routine was to go from
summer school then back home and, on
some weekends, to the swimming pool. It
went kind of fast, and before I knew it, the
regular school session had started.

By this time I was about five months
pregnant, so they wouldn't let me attend a
public school. They sent me to Emerson,
which was an alternative school and not just
for pregnant girls but for anyone who

couldn't attend regular school. It was horrible. The teachers seemed to not want to be there, and the students surely didn't want to be there, so it was one big mess.

Bullies roamed the hallways and made their presence known on the school bus. It was not fun. So I decided that as soon as I got off the school bus, I would walk to the library downtown and read all day, then head back to school to catch the bus home—an hour walk there and an hour walk back. At least I got my exercise.

I tried to keep a low profile and not deal with anyone, but you know that's just not good enough for some people. There were two Hispanic girls who acted as if they had been born simply to pick at me, call me names, or poke fun at me.

A person can only take so much, pregnant or not. I think I was about six and a half months along, so I was no longer able to hide it. They got off the bus at my stop and just started picking at me. Needless to say, they caught me on the wrong day, and, believe it or not, I forgot all about being

214

pregnant. I grabbed one by her hair, wrapped my hands in it, and used her as a shield while I hit at the other.

My mind kind of blanked out, because the next thing I remember, they were running in the other direction. I made my way home with a bloody nose and a split lip but, all in all, unscathed. They let me be after that, and if I saw them in school, they would always walk in the opposite direction.

My temper wasn't the best on any given day as it was, but add hormones into the equation and you had a recipe for disaster. I was told that as long as I didn't keep my temper in check, I couldn't go to the group home for unwed mothers. There was only one in OKC, and at any given time it only accepted five mothers and their babies. They couldn't have an emotionally out-of-control and unstable person around the babies. So, guess what? I actually managed to get it together and was finally able to go to the home.

On January 19, 1989, at Oklahoma Memorial Hospital at 8:26 a.m., Marcus

Tyrone Nelson made his appearance in this world after twenty-three and a half hours of labor and a C-section. I was way too tired to think of a name, even though I had been trying to decide for months, so I named him after the hero in a book I was reading (*Velvet Lightning*, by Kay Hooper).

He weighed six pounds, four ounces and was nineteen and three-quarters inches long. I was terrified. I stayed in the hospital for over a week because I had a uterine infection. I felt like I was dying. I just knew it was the medication they were giving me.

217

These people were trying to kill me. (I had such a wild imagination.) I kept threatening to take the IV out. One of the nurses leaned down and whispered in my ear that if I took it out I was going to bleed to death and die. Well, of course I didn't want to die, so I calmed the heck down. Finally, we went home, but I was so clueless. Marcus wasn't a bad baby; I just didn't know what I was doing.

He cried all the time, and then I cried all the time, and we just cried together. No matter how much I fed him, he wasn't gaining a lot of weight, and they started looking at me like I was doing something wrong. It was too much. Because I was a ward of the state and was underage, Marcus should have become a ward of the state too. But Andrea told me that if I could find somebody to take care of him with no help from the state, they wouldn't take him into custody.

There was only one person I thought to ask. That was my foster mother Georgia Roberson in Inola, and she said yes without evening thinking. So at six months, Marcus went to Inola, and I went back to the shelter

219

until Andrea could find me another

placement. That time in the shelter, I met a

young girl, Brenda. We became best friends.

She was the sister I never had. We told each

other everything, no matter what. We ran

away together and had each other's back.

I also found out that she was the sister of the

guy I had a crush on when I lived at A. J.'s

home. Nobody liked Brenda but me. I

couldn't understand why, though. The day

came, however, that they found a foster

home for her. I cried because my best friend

was leaving me, but we swore that we would

220

write each other. I had lost my best friend and my son all within a few months of each other. I visited him as much as I could, but there was no doubt he was loved very much by everyone in Inola.

Because I was sixteen, they couldn't find a foster home placement for me, so they sent me to Job Corps in McKinney, Texas, which was probably not the best idea my caseworker ever had.

The McKinney Job Corps was for people sixteen to twenty-four years old and was a closed center, which meant everyone had to live there. Another bad idea. Job Corps was kind of a culture shock to me. I had no real supervision; nobody was looking over my shoulder telling me what I could and couldn't do. So I'm pretty sure I lost my mind for a little bit. The first night I was there, I ran into my soon-to-be boyfriend.

Remember what I said about that darn apple falling from the tree? This was the first and thankfully the only physically abusive relationship I was ever in. His name was

Lawrence, but everybody at Job Corps called him Al Capone.

I probably should have run in the opposite direction, but apparently I had a thing for bad boys. Job Corps was like a little town. Everybody knew everybody's business, and even though you were there to learn and get a trade, that wasn't what it was like. McKinney was a dry town, but that didn't stop the alcohol from getting onto the Job Corps campus, and since there weren't any rules in place to stop it, you could get alcohol no matter the cost. The easy access

223

almost turned me into an alcoholic at sixteen years old.

Since Capone was the campus bully, I never had any friends, because everyone was afraid of him. Hell, I was scared of him. He used to hit me a lot, but never any place on my body where anyone could see. He controlled my every move, and after I got out of my classes, I had to be in my dorm unless he was with me, and if I didn't listen, he would hit me.

I wasn't mentally ready to be at Job Corps, being sixteen and dealing with older personalities. I was doomed from the beginning…I think.

Fighting, drinking, and getting high—that was my every day and weekend. After a while my classwork began to suffer, until I was skipping all the time and just hanging out. Lawrence took what little self-esteem I had and crushed it to bits. I was alone on a downward spiral with no one to turn to, and then I got my first letter from Howard.

He was an older cousin from California who started writing to me. Those letters caused great contention between Lawrence and me, but they were a lifeline for me, and for a little while, I felt like I meant something to somebody. Lawrence tore a few up because he knew how much they meant to me. He wasn't happy unless I had no one to turn to.

Then the inevitable happened. Yes, you guessed it: I ended up pregnant. I had a miscarriage, though. With all the pressure and emotional trauma this brought on, I ran away from Job Corps and hitchhiked a ride

226

to Oakland, California—clearly not learning the lesson from my last hitchhiking event, but hoping I made it safely.

I hadn't seen any of my family for eight years, so I decided to go. Good thing God watches out for kids like me, because I did make it safely, and I got to see my brothers, aunts, and cousins. That trip was also the last time that I got to see my grandma before she died.

This was the first time that I had hitchhiked that distance alone. I didn't have the sense to

be scared. I packed my bag and hit the road.
Getting off the Job Corps grounds was easy;
getting out of McKinney—well, not so
much. It seemed as if I walked forever
before I was able to get somebody to stop
and give me a ride. Finally, after I swear my
feet were about to fall off, someone did stop
for me and gave me a ride into Dallas. That
person dropped me off downtown at the bus
station, and from there I jumped back on the
freeway and started walking again.

As the sun was starting to rise, this white
man pulled onto the side of the highway and

228

beckoned me to get in. I threw my bag in the backseat of his car and hopped in the front seat, just happy to be off my feet for a while.

As he started going, he asked me where I was headed. I told him I was going to Oakland to see my family. When he asked me how old I was, of course I lied. I told him I was eighteen. His look told me he didn't believe me, but he didn't call me an out-and-out liar to my face. He just said that he had a little sister my age and that he wouldn't want her traveling these streets.

He was an army ranger on leave, and he could take me as far as Arizona. Boy, was I happy. On our drive he fed me and preached the dangers of a young girl hitchhiking across the world alone. As we made it to Arizona, you could tell he was worried about leaving me. As we crossed the state line, there was a car on the side of the road with smoke coming from underneath the hood, so of course he just had to pull over and help. There were two Asian ladies looking under the hood, clueless. He moved them aside and started looking under the hood. Apparently one of the hoses had burst.

He asked where they were headed, and they told him Berkeley, California. He told them he would be more than happy to fix their problem. So he drove to the auto store, got the part, and put it on, and they were road-ready in less than an hour. They offered to pay him. He told them if they could take me to Oakland to my family, that would be payment enough. And they said yes. As he put my bag in their car, he pushed fifty dollars into my hand and told me to be safe.

231

I got in the car with the women. They didn't speak much to me on the long drive, but they did get me to my destination safely. They dropped me off at the Oakland airport, where I called my brother to come get me. I was so excited to see my big brother. It didn't matter to me that I hadn't seen or spoke to him in over ten years. He was my brother, and he was coming. I went home with him until the next day. When I got up, of course the first thing I did was call Andrea. She was not happy with me, but she said she would start working on

transportation to get me back to Tulsa.

So in the meantime, I went to see all the

family I hadn't seen since I was five: my

grandma, my aunts, my cousin. I was in

heaven—until my aunt asked out of the blue,

"So where are you going to stay? Because

you can't stay here." I remember feeling

hurt and angry—angry because I never even

asked to stay with anybody in the first place.

At least let me ask before you say no. And I

was hurt because here was someone else of

my blood not wanting me—rejection.

233

I remember looking in the mirror, staring at
myself, trying to see what my family saw,
what was so wrong with me that nobody
could love me and nobody wanted me.

That was the last time I saw my
grandmother. She died a few years later.
Andrea got me a flight back to Tulsa forty-
eight hours after I called her. So back to the
shelter I went. Wouldn't you know that
Andrea pulled all kind of strings and got me
back in Job Corps?

When I went back, I just didn't care. I went
into a deep depression. I was so tired of
feeling like I was so unwanted. So what did
I do? I got back with Lawrence. I can't even
tell you what I was thinking. He was hateful
and abusive, mentally and physically, but on
the inside I felt that that was all I was worth,
and wouldn't you know I got pregnant
again. He got kicked out of Job Corps for his
behavior, and I got kicked out for fighting.
So back to Tulsa and the shelter I went.
Andrea was so upset with me, and when I

told her I was pregnant, you could see the disappointment written on her face.

Hell, I was kind of disappointed in myself. What was I going to do with another baby? I couldn't take care of the one I had. I couldn't even take care of me. I could feel myself becoming a statistic.

So when the subject of abortion was brought up, I didn't say no. I remember the morning Andrea took me to get the procedure. We pulled up to the clinic. There were about thirty people outside the building with signs.

## Some Hurts Are Beyond Tears

She told me that when we walked up the
sidewalk that I should look straight ahead,
not look any of them in the eyes, not look at
the signs and ignore everything they were
saying.

It's kind of hard to ignore people when
they're yelling things like "You're a baby
murderer," "You're going to burn in hell"
and so forth. I made it into the building
physically unscathed but emotionally numb.
I honestly felt nothing. I wasn't nervous. I
was just numb. I don't think I fully
comprehended the choice I was making.

And if I had known that this would be the last time I would carry a child, would I have chosen differently? I guess that's a lot to ask anybody, much less a sixteen-year-old child.

I had the procedure and pushed it into one of those places in my mind where I put all things that hurt too much to dwell on. I was good at that. I went back to the shelter, and when I got there, guess who was back: Brenda. I had missed her so much. We hugged and laughed and talked all night, getting caught up. We stayed put for a good two weeks before we hit the streets again for

two weeks. She kept my mind off my pain.
Then they found her another placement.
After a month of feeling down because my
friend had left, I started to get itchy feet
again.

So I went AWOL with one of my other
friends, Montishi whom I had met while in
the shelter. It was the weekend, and we were
just walking around the north side of Tulsa
until this car pulled up beside us and called
out her name. The driver asked us where we
were going, and we said, "Nowhere." He
told us to get in the car with him; we could

hang with him that night. My friend
introduced us. His name was Shawn, but he
said everybody called him "Sugar Look"
because he looked so sweet. Can you say
"corny"? But I guess when you're cute you
can pull off corny.

So we went home with him. He fed us. We
watched TV. He plied us with liquor. My
friend went to sleep, and I stayed up and
talked to Shawn. We talked about his son,
how he wanted to get out of Tulsa, how he
wanted to find someone to settle down with
and raise his son. Now, mind you, I was

240

sixteen, almost seventeen, and he was nineteen. We talked and fooled around right into sex. I probably should have felt bad and cheap about sleeping with somebody I had just met, but honestly, by then I just wanted to feel wanted and loved.

That's how I equated sex in my mind. I was looking for love and validation in all the wrong ways. So the next day I was thinking, "Oh, he really likes me," until I found out he already had a girlfriend. Can you say "crushed"?

Montishi and I went back to the shelter, cleaned up, ate, took a nap, and went AWOL again, but this time we had a destination. This time she wanted to go see this boy she liked. His name was Jayson. I swear the whole walk there was Jayson this and Jayson that.

"Oh, Jayson is so cute, Jayson is so sweet." I was about sick of hearing about Jayson. As we got closer to our destination, she told me that Jayson worked at his father's liquor store, but he worked in the back, where his dad had made a little snack store so the kids would have a place to buy little snacks. As we were walking by, the side door opened up, and out walked one of the cutest boys I had ever seen. He walked up to me as bold as you could be, threw his arm over my shoulder, and said, "Hey, my name is Cardell, and I'm going to be your boyfriend." I have to say I was very flattered.

He then proceeded to ask me out on a date. A real date. I told him I would like that, but I had people with me. He told me not to worry, because he would find them dates

too, and he was going to pay for everything.
So my two friends Keisha and Montishi and
his two friends ended up going to the movies
and the Waffle House afterward. I have to
say I really believe those three boys were the
reason the Waffle House stopped doing all
you can eat.

They could eat! After the meal we all went
back to Cardell's house and hung out in his
room, laughing and getting to know each
other. About 4:00 a.m. Cardell took us girls
back to the shelter. As we were all getting
out of his truck, he stopped me and told me

244

that he would like to see me again but

without my friends. I said sure, so he said

he'd be back that night after the liquor store

closed. He said he would be in the parking

lot across the street and playing his music

real loud so I'd know he was there. I was so

giddy with excitement and nervous all day.

What if he didn't come? What if he did? He

showed up at 9:30 p.m., and I hit the shelter

door running. I jumped into his truck, and he

peeled off. We went to eat, and we went for

a drive, and we talked. He told me about his

family. I told him about how I came to be in

the shelter. Not everything, though—I didn't want to run him off. He took me back to the shelter after our drive and said he wanted to come get me again Sunday after he got out of church.

He wanted to take me to dinner. (I swear, that boy loved to eat.) I was so excited. He really seemed to like me, and I liked him too. So on our first real date alone, he took me to the Louisiana Boiling Pot.

We had to wear these funky little bibs, and since he ordered for us both, they came and dumped a pot full of red bugs in front of us.

Needless to say, I was horrified. He called

them crawfish. I called them what they

were: boiled bugs. Their beady little eyes

were looking at me.

There was no way in the world I was eating

that stuff. Not to seem ungrateful or

anything, but I'd rather have had a burger.

Other than that, the date went well. After

"dinner" (I use that word loosely), we went

for a drive.

I asked him where we were going, and he said he wanted to go check on his cousin and that that way his two favorite people could meet. I thought that was so cute and sweet—until we started driving through a neighborhood that was so familiar. We were driving down the same street that Shawn lived on, where Montishi and I had spent the night two weeks before.

My heart was in my throat. I kept praying to myself, "Please, no. Please do not pull up in front of this boy's house." But of course he did, and I about passed out right then, right there.

But thankfully Shawn wasn't there. So we drove back to Cardell's house, where I spent the night, and all I could think was, "This is not going to end well at all." The next morning Cardell dropped me off back at the shelter.

For weeks that's how it went: he would come scoop me up from the shelter, and we would spend all our time together. It was wonderful. I was so happy and in love. But with one phone call, all that came to a screeching halt.

We were sitting in Cardell's room, just laughing and talking, when the phone rang. There was no reason, but as soon as the phone rang, my stomach dropped. I just knew that this was it—the phone call I had been dreading. I wasn't disappointed. It was Shawn on the other end. I was sitting so close to Cardell that I could hear both sides of the conversation. Shawn asked Cardell where he had been, because he hadn't seen him around.

250

Cardell told him he had found a girlfriend,

that we had been hanging, and that he

wanted Shawn to meet me.

Shawn was like, "Cool. What's her name?"

When Cardell said my name, I couldn't

listen anymore. I knew what was coming, so

I walked out the door and went and sat on

the porch. The first thing Cardell said was,

"How could you? How could you sleep with

my cousin and not tell me?"

I scrambled for any excuse but the truth.

How could I tell him the truth? I was so

messed up in the head that the slightest bit

of affection from anybody made me feel

special and loved, and I wanted that feeling

so much that if I had to sleep with somebody

to get it, so be it. So I lied.

I told him that the only reason I slept with

Shawn was that I found out the foster home

I was supposed to go to didn't pass its home

test, and the reason I didn't tell him about

Shawn was that I didn't want him to look at

me differently. I guess there was some truth

in that. I wanted him to see me as special,

and if he had known what I had done, I

didn't think he'd want to be with me
anymore.

He made me feel wanted and loved, and
after not having that for so long, I didn't
want to lose it. He took me back to the
shelter. I got out of his truck not really
knowing where our relationship stood. So I
assumed the worst. The next day Andrea
came to tell me that they had found a foster-
care placement for me.

This placement was horrible. They weren't
the nicest or the cleanest people. My new

253

foster mother was so nice when Andrea was there, but as soon as she left, the real her came out. She worked a lot, but her husband didn't. He was tremendously overweight, so all he did was sit on the couch, watch television, and eat. Oh, and did I mention he was a pervert?

After I was there a few weeks, he started saying inappropriate things about my breasts and butt and how if he were younger, he knew what he would do to keep a girl like me in check—on my back with some hard dick stuffed up in me. I politely told him that if he ever touched me, I would stab him in it and watch him bleed out.

His wife liked to point out how grateful I should feel that she and her husband had welcomed me into their home when no one else wanted me.

I was so sick of hearing that, so I told her, "Look, I'm doing you a favor by staying, since your lazy, fat-ass husband won't get off his butt and go to work. The money you get for keeping me I'm sure comes in handy." I then turned around, went into the room that my presence paid for, shut the

door, and started plotting my escape.

I called Cardell, but he didn't answer. Our

relationship hadn't been the same since the

whole Shawn debacle. It was really strained.

One day about a week later, there was a

knock at the door. My foster father was in

the den on the couch, where he nearly

always was, and my foster mother was gone,

so I went and answered the door. When I

opened it, I was dumbstruck to see who was

standing there. What the heck was Shawn

doing there, and how did he even find out where I was?

I asked him. He told me Cardell had told him where I lived now. Now, why in the world would he do that? He told me that that didn't matter. What mattered was the reason he was there, which was that he couldn't stop thinking about me. Why did I just leave his house like that?

He thought we had connected. Now, even I'm not that dumb. It had setup written all over it. But of course I stood there and listened. And the sad thing is that I wanted to believe him so much, even though I knew what he was selling was garbage. Something inside me wanted to feel that I was too important to let go.

He had his say; gave me his number; and told me if I ever needed him, he would always be there for me. Even if he had been telling the truth, he still would have left me, because he died five year later in a tragic accident.

## Some Hurts Are Beyond Tears

The fact of the matter is that the people you

love and care for will always leave you,

willingly or unwillingly. But I digress. I

went up to Cardell's job and confronted him.

I asked him, "Why would you send Shawn

to my house?" Of course he denied doing so,

but we both knew there was no other way

for him to have known where I lived.

So I let him stick to his lie, and he pretended

like I believed him. After a few months, the

new foster home crashed and burned, so I

was back to the shelter. In my mind the

shelter was the safest place for me. Nobody

tried to belittle me; nobody tried to touch or

molest me or take from me what I wasn't

willing to give. They cared about me. Well,

most of them, anyway. There was always

Tony, with his mean and hateful self. Once

again I went AWOL, and once again Tony

was on duty when I came back, and once

again it was cold, and once again he

wouldn't let me come in. So I trudged up to

Hillcrest hospital and sat in the emergency

room to warm up and to call Cardell, but he

wasn't answering his home phone or his

pager. So I did what I hadn't allowed myself

to do for months: I called Shawn. He

answered. I asked him if he knew where

Cardell was. He asked me why I wanted to

know, and I told him that I couldn't get back

in the shelter and that I didn't have any

place to go. He asked me where I was, so I

told him. He said he was on his way to pick

me up. He came and got me, took me back

to his house, fed me, and warmed me up.

Then he proceeded to tell me that Cardell

was messing with some other girl; that's

why he wasn't answering any of my pages

(back when we had pagers). I told him he

was lying. Cardell wasn't like that; he was probably at home, sleeping.

His reply was, "Why would I lie?"

I told him, "Because you want to get in my drawers."

He told me he had already been there, so he didn't have a reason to lie.

You know that moment when you know you're being played but just can't figure out how and why? He told me to just watch Cardell, ask questions, and really listen to the answers. Well, about two days later, I decided to confront Cardell. I would pick a day he had been drinking heavily. I asked him if he was cheating on me, and the argument was on. In the middle of our argument, he pulled out a pistol he always kept in his truck and put it against my head and told me he was going to shoot me. I don't know if I thought he was serious or not, but I remember saying to him, "Don't shoot me in the head. Shoot me in the shoulder." He told me he loved me too much for me to suffer, so he would just make it quick. Then he pulled the trigger. I'm pretty

sure I peed on myself. The gun wasn't
loaded. He pushed me away from him and
told me not to ever question him. He
dropped me back off at the shelter.

I said to myself, "Self, he's crazier than a
betsey bug and you need to leave him
alone." So what did I do? I called Shawn
and told him what had happened. Of course
he just had to come comfort me, and I let
him.

Two days later Cardell showed up at the
shelter. I ran out and got into his truck. He

apologized and told me how sorry he was

and that it would never happen again. I

didn't know what to do. I was caught up in

them both. They both gave me something I

thought I was missing. I was seventeen, with

no self-esteem and looking toward others to

make me feel good about myself. Sex wasn't

special to me. It didn't mean anything, not

the act itself. It was the rest that made me

feel something—the holding-me part, the

part where I felt protected and safe in strong

arms, even if it was just for a little while,

even if it was all a lie.

I'm not proud of what I did, but, then, I just didn't care. I just wanted to feel worth something to somebody. I believed my stepfather was right all those years ago. This would be all that boys and men would want from me Over the next year, I was in and out of so many foster homes I can't even remember them all. Through this transition I lost contact with Cardell and Shawn. Finally, somehow or other, my aunt Vergie was able to get me. For years I thought my aunt didn't like me, so in my mind I wondered why she would even take me in.

But then I thought, "Of *course*—for the money." We lived with my cousins Boobie and Vanessa in a small duplex. But I have to admit there were good times there. My aunt got them to let me back in school. She was very adamant about doing my schoolwork and not fighting. I wish she could have been there before my mind got all twisted up. I went to Will Rogers High School. Boobie would take me and pick me up from school. She was the best cousin. She even drove me and my little boyfriend around.

Everything was going so well for those few months—and then everything went to hell in a handbasket, all because some girl just had to show the world she was a bad chick, and of course she picked me to show out on. I was trying to stay out of trouble and do want my aunt Vergie told me to do. But, hey, I was never one to back away from a fight. I accidentally knocked over her books in the annex building. I even apologized and picked them up, but she had to show out in front of her friends. She started talking loudly until she drew a crowd, calling me all kind of names, telling me I "wasn't nobody" and how I thought I was so cute. (I have to admit I was kind of cute that day.)

I had on this white button-down shirt with a blue-and-black plaid skirt with suspenders—not really fighting attire. I could have walked away. Hell, I might have walked away, but we'll never know, because this chick reached all the way back and slapped me right in the face. For a split second, all I could do was stare at her, and then the old me kicked in. I grabbed that girl by her long hair, wrapped it around both my hands, and proceeded to make her head hit every locker on that floor of the building. I dragged her!

If you control the head, you control the body. It took two grown male teachers to separate me from her head, and I'm pretty sure she was half-bald from their efforts. Of course they called my aunt, and she was livid. I tried to tell her that I didn't start it, but she wasn't listening. She said she sent me to school to learn not to fight. She told me I was grounded. Right then I knew I wouldn't be staying; this wasn't going to work. She wasn't hearing me.

So that night I sneaked out the window. I learned years later that she knew what had really happened, and if I would have heard her instead of the voices in my head, things might have turned out differently. So back into the shelter I went. And guess who was there? Yep, Brenda.

We didn't really run away much. We talked a lot about how I wanted to do stuff for my son but didn't have any money. So I sneaked off and got a job at Sonic, my first real job. The staff at the shelter would sneak me to work and sneak me back in just so I could

271

make some extra money to get my baby
something for his birthday.

I finally got paid, and I was so excited. I told
Brenda the next day I was going to go
AWOL and buy him some tennis shoes. She
seemed to be happy for me as we went to
bed.

The next morning when I woke up, Brenda
was gone, and so was the money. I was so
mad I couldn't see straight. I just knew that
when I got my hands on her, I was going to

choke her with my bare hands. How could

she be my best friend and steal from me?

If she had needed something, I would have

given it to her. If I had it, she had it. I felt so

betrayed. I knew, though, that all I had to do

was be patient. I'd get my chance. Pretty

soon they found me a placement. After a

few weeks, though, I was back in the shelter

again. That foster home didn't last long at

all. While I was AWOL from the shelter, I

went to one of my favorite places, the

downtown library. Books had a calming

effect on me.

While I was down there, I ran across some

friends who said Brenda had been saying

that when she saw me, she was going to beat

my butt! Really? You steal from me and my

baby, but you're going to fight me? OK,

game on. After asking the right questions,

Montishi, another girl I use to run around

with (Montishi tried to jump bad with me

once, until I hung her out the window by her

feet, with every intention of letting her drop

from the second floor. Joe saved her. After

that, though, we were the best of friends for

some reason.) found out where she was. She

274

was holed up with some guy about four blocks from the shelter, behind Hillcrest hospital. So Montishi and I headed that way. I went and knocked on the door. Brenda asked who it was, and I told her. She wouldn't come out. I hollered through the door, "You said you were going to beat my butt when you saw me, so I thought I'd make it easy on you. Here I am." But of course she wouldn't open the door.

I told Montishi to go around back and climb through the window. If Brenda wasn't going to come out and fight me, I was going to go in and fight her. (I'm pretty sure we were

breaking all kinds of laws.) Montishi finally

got in the apartment and opened up the door

for me. I walked up to Brenda and slapped

her. I told her that was for taking the money

for my son's shoes! Then I said, "I heard

you were going to beat my butt when you

saw me. You've seen me now. Beat my

ass." She just looked at me with tears in her

eyes, which pissed me off more, because

then I was feeling guilty. She did me wrong,

Why was I the one feeling guilty? No matter

how many times I hit her, she wouldn't hit me back.

I told Montishi to go get a jug of soapy water, and I dragged Brenda outside and told her to take off all her clothes. (Mind you, it was February in Tulsa—freezing weather.) I picked up a stick and told her again to take off all her clothes. I let her keep on her shoes, and then I poured the jug of water on her and told her to start walking butt naked. I made her walk eight blocks in the cold with just her shoes on. I told her to go up to the shelter door and ring the doorbell. The thing is, at the shelter, anytime you ring the doorbell, all the kids run to the window to see who the police are bringing in, and during the day everybody is in the main building.

So when she rang that doorbell, everybody came running—staff and kids alike. Once they saw Brenda, Shaundra ran and got her a blanket to cover up.

When I went back to the shelter later that day, they sent me to the detention center, where I was charged with strong-arm

278

robbery. They said I robbed her of her clothes by intimidation. I had to write her a formal apology, telling her how sorry I was.

The judge told me they could keep me in the system until I was twenty-one. I'm pretty sure that was an empty threat, but I didn't want to take any chances. So I wrote the apology.

I was almost eighteen; where had the time gone? Ten years of bad decisions, ten years of hurting myself and allowing others to hurt me. Ten years of watching those who were supposed to love me cause me undue pain.

My experiences had shaped the way I thought and felt. Now I had to take all the lessons I'd learned over the years and put them to use in the real world. I have to say that I was poorly equipped to handle adult life. As I stepped out to take my place in life, I felt all kinds of emotions: fear of the unknown, uncertainty about how was I going to make it, relief that I was still here when many of those I had known hadn't made it that far. They weren't given the chance to live this thing called life. I was as ready as I would ever be.

If I had only known that in some ways, the next ten years would be worse than the first. That I was a statistic waiting to happen. But God had his hand on me and was protecting me through the pain, the hurt, and the bad decisions that I would make over the years.

God had a purpose for my life. I just had to find it, and when I found it, the cycle that had become a part of my life would be broken, and I would see that there was

indeed a purpose for my pain.

Made in the USA
Monee, IL
23 January 2024